YOUR
LIFE'S
CALLING

YOUR LIFE'S CALLING

getting unstuck
and fulfilling
your life lessons

BY NANCY CANNING

Canning, Nancy
Your life's calling: getting unstuck and fulfilling your life lessons /
Nancy Canning, M.A. – 1st ed.

ISBN: Paperback: 978-0-9823661-2-7
ISBN: Ebook: 978-0-9823661-3-4
1.   Mind and body 2. Self-help 3. Self-actualization 4. Title

1st edition, October 2014

Printed in the United States of America

ALSO BY NANCY CANNING, M.A.

Books:

Past to Present: How Your Past Lives Are Impacting You Now

Co-Author: *The Inspiration Bible: The Unseen Force Transforming Lives Worldwide*

CDs – available on author's web site www.NancyCanning.com:

Past Life Regression

Relax Now

CDs to help you transform your limiting belief systems:

Transform "I'm Not Worthy, Don't Deserve"

Transform "I Worry, Doubt, Don't Trust"

Transform "I'm Stuck/Procrastinate"

Transform "I'm Not Enough"

Transform Your Finances

Transform Your Self Image

Transform Your Self Confidence

Transform To Your Ideal Weight

Transform Your Eating Habits

Change Any Belief

With deep love and gratitude for my family,

Dick and Peggy Canning,

Barbara, Art, Susan and Bob

ACKNOWLEDGEMENTS

This book wouldn't have come into physical manifestation without my personal "village," to whom I am deeply grateful:

- To my sister, Barbara McNurlin, for your loving and consistent editorial help, for believing in me and my work, and for keeping me on track,

- To all of you who helped me through the ups and downs of changing my own beliefs: Janet Rogers Brides, Dr. Kim Jobst, Jon Robson, Dr. John Demartini, Dr. Joseph Spear, and the many other healers, therapists, and energy workers over the years,

- To my incredible friends. You have encouraged me through all your love, your kind words, and your never-ending support,

- For your marketing ideas and suggestions for getting this book distributed on a wider scale, Rita Ramsay and Sue McClanahan,

- To my mastermind leader, Felicia Searcy, and the women in my group, Mauree, Laney, Joan, Joanne, and JT. The consistency of our weekly coaching calls has kept me motivated and helped me through to this finished product, and

- To all my clients throughout the years. Your courage and willingness to delve deeply into your own limiting beliefs has inspired me, helped me grow and change, and has enabled me to become the person I am today. Without you, this book would not have been possible.

FOREWORD

We shall not cease from exploration,
And the end of all our exploring,
Will be to arrive where we started
And know the place for the first time.
T.S. Elliott *Little Gidding*

What is Life?

Yes/No seriously, I do indeed mean to ask that question! Surely, every one of us asks that question at some stage in our lives, some of us often. In some, as in me, it is insistent, driving every aspect of life day after day, moment by moment, affecting every choice, decision, and conversation. It is the force that impels me to serve and to explore, to heal and to be healed. At times, its impact exquisitely delicious, bringing an appreciation of intimate relatedness, of Oneness with all life, whether or not in relationship. At others, its impact an excruciating, searing pain, an incessant pointed and agonising pressure relentlessly impinging on every waking moment, and even, it seems, in sleep and dreams.

In the trajectory that is my life, this question has never left me — and the more I live, the more I experience, the deeper I go, living, loving, exploring, with ever more gratitude, the more remarkable is what emerges – the more beautiful, the more awe-inspiring, the more miraculous, no matter how challenging is the question and what it gives rise to. Right now, and for the foreseeable future, Nancy Canning, the author of this book, is part and parcel of that question – certainly in this lifetime and who knows, may be in many others too.

I am fortunate beyond words to have been introduced to Nancy and in coming to know her personally and professionally, to trust her as I do, even though we have not yet met in person. I have gained immeasurably, as have countless other people as a result, most of those having no idea the sources that have contributed to the gifts being manifested and shared.

It is interesting how these things happen. A simple introduction to Nancy with the gift of a session with her on Skype, came through a much respected colleague and friend, Dr. Jenny Remington-Hobbs. In no way could I have known what that introduction would lead to for us all. This book is, in part, a result, as you will discover, and I am humbled to have played even a small part in the odyssey that has been Nancy's life. This is a book that will, without a shadow of doubt, assist those searching for meaning, searching to understand, to find more of that ever elusive and ever changing answer to the ever present niggle inside that *there is more to know*, to become, that there is ever more to find, to embrace, to encompass, to understand and to experience about this extraordinary life that each one of us has, AND ESPECIALLY SO when things are really, really tough, emotionally harrowing and nothing seems to make sense.

I am a Physician, Scientist, Healer, Husband, Father, Lover, Friend, a Human being on The Way. In my work, what I love to do is to go behind the symptoms, underneath them, deep inside the being of my clients to discover what their life force is seeking to express and communicate to and for them and everyone else. And I do this so that people might experience, even if only for a moment, the Divine Magnificence of Life itself, however it is expressing itself through them at any given moment. The content of this book has helped me profoundly as it has others. Working with Nancy one-on-one on Skype is a deeply privileged experience, for Nancy's work is an expression of her relentless search for authenticity, integrity and understanding. This book is a part of the incredible service she has done and will go on to do for millions of people world-wide.

Your Life's Calling is beautifully written – in a way that can only happen when the author really knows her stuff, when the author is writing from the heart, an open heart that has suffered the path to discovery and enlightenment, through years of committed professional and personal experience, and has decided to expand and Love instead of becoming bitter and diminishing in stature. Dip in to this book or read it cover to cover – do whatever you are drawn to do. Bring to it whatever question you have about what things mean in your life. Bring to it your pains, your sufferings, your questions, all of them the products of your uncontrolled mind and emotions, and work with it, starting wherever you wish. Very few will put the book down without having gained something.

This book is an Aladdin's cave of practical treasure and if you read it right, savouring the insights and exercises, deceptively simply articulated, a genie will emerge from the writings to assist you to solve your existential and psychological problems if such is your wish! I will be amazed if you do not find meaning and support for just your specific problem – as though it had been written just for you. This is such a book. I am overjoyed to have this book to give to my clients – it is a book that is much needed for all the therapeutic disciplines. It is a book that enables "functional shift" in people, a book that can facilitate cure for Diseases of Meaning. This is a book that will really help people.

Dr. Kim A. Jobst MA DM MRCP MFHom
Physician, Healer and Teacher.
London and Hereford. UK
www.functionalshift.com

Dr. Kim A. Jobst is a Consultant Physician in Integrated Medicine with specialist accreditation in General Internal Medicine and Neurodegenerative Diseases and Dementia. He has Specialist Training as a Medical Homoeopath, completed a Jungian Training Analysis, trained in traditional Chinese Acupuncture, is a trained Demartini facilitator, and has worked with Foodstate Nutritional supplementation and lifestyle interventions for many years. He is Editor-in Chief of the peer reviewed, scientific *Journal of Alternative and Complementary Medicine: Research on Paradigm, Practice and Policy* and author and co-author of over 150 scientific papers.

TABLE OF CONTENTS

1

Begin Where You Are

The fact that you are reading this book is a miracle.

It's a miracle that this book even exists because it has taken many years and tears, and much therapy and healing, to get me beyond my limiting thoughts and beliefs to bring this work to you in physical form. I've carried it in my mind for over a decade.

But I've been stuck. Now, happily, I'm unstuck.

If you feel stuck in any part of your life, perhaps my story will help you become unstuck as well – to live your life doing what you really want to do.

MY STORY

In a nutshell, here's my "I can't bring myself to write this book" story. I began writing it several times, only to stop and put it away. I took writing courses. I have friends who buy writing books, read them, and are grateful for the insights and techniques they learn. However, I did not buy books about how to write because I knew I wouldn't read them. So I did that correctly, for me.

In 2013, I spent six weeks in sunny and warm California to get out of Massachusetts' cold winter and to write this book – and not return home until it was done. I shipped my files across the country and I began writing. I even took a daylong writing class and had a session with a writing coach. I wrote parts of different chapters.

But then, I stopped writing. I felt lost, not sure of the direction I was to go. I'd had clear ideas, but the session with a writing coach left me feeling discouraged and on the wrong track. I really wanted the book written, but I didn't have the resiliency to continue writing. All my plans and desires faded into the background. I ended up simply enjoying my family in the warm California winter weather.

But my dream had not died; it had just gone dormant. Six months later, in the fall, I enrolled in a coaching program and have received weekly help ever since. I attended a weekend conference in January 2014 where I gained more clarity on my vision for this book….yet, I still had no desire to write.

This year, 2014, I again came to California to escape the brutal winter in New England, to spend time with family, and to write. But instead of writing, I only glanced at my client files as I walked by them. There they sat, in the shipped box. I'd briefly look at what I'd already written in the computer, and then would move on to "important" work…like answering emails, or surfing the Internet. I didn't even try to write. It felt like an obligation and I just couldn't do it.

I've done a lot of work on my limiting beliefs. I've had help from colleagues. But I couldn't get to the core of what was keeping me from writing – until today.

In California, I have been doing deep therapeutic work to change my underlying beliefs and resolve the emotional underpinnings that keep me from doing what I truly want to do: write this book. Ta da, this life changing work has done the job. I'll give more details later. Suffice it to say here that I have changed my thinking and now I'm writing. To me, that's a miracle!

What is a miracle? According to the book *A Course In Miracles*, a miracle is a shift in perception. That means: a shift in how you see life; a shift in the meaning you put on an event; a shift in your thinking; a shift in your emotional reactions of certain strongly held beliefs; a shift in your behaviors.

In order to begin writing, continue writing, finish writing, and publish this book, I had to shift many of my perceptions about myself, my abilities, and my view of the world.

For me, my journey of creating this book is no different than the journey all of us are on in our daily lives. For those of us on the path of becoming and being all that we can be, our life journey is about changing our limiting perceptions, shifting to more empowering beliefs, growing into a higher consciousness, and taking different actions.

The purpose of our journey is to move toward whatever calls us from inside to be happy, to achieve our dreams, to accomplish our heart's desires, to quench our soul's yearning. But we encounter challenges and obstacles that appear to stand in our way of actually achieving these accomplishments.

Surprisingly, these obstacles are often of our own making. Literally, we make them up in our minds. We don't intentionally create them for ourselves. No, rather, we create them from the subconscious limiting beliefs we have carried since childhood.

I knew I had deeply held "childish" beliefs that kept me stuck, that would not let me write this book. I also knew I had to dig deeply enough to uncover them and replace them with "adult" beliefs that would shift my perspective and support my adult desire to write.

What do I know about shifting perceptions? Why am I writing about this subject? The short answer is that I'm at expert at this work. I've been helping people shift their thinking since 1980, when I first learned about "belief systems." You might think, from my description of my non-writing journey above, that I sure don't know much about the subject because I've had such a winding road to get to the finished project. Right?

My colleagues and I often discuss this apparent paradox amongst ourselves. It's the phenomenon of "healer, heal thyself." It's one of the aspects of our work that is most agonizing. We can help others absolutely change their perspectives and create miracles in their lives. Yet, we can be just as stumped by our own "stuff" as our clients are with theirs. This I know for sure: We are all on the journey of self-discovery and growth and none of us is immune from the effects of our limiting beliefs...until we shift them.

For me, though, being stuck as a hypnotherapist has brought me numerous benefits.

One, it keeps my ego in check. It's hard to be egotistical, thinking "I've got it all together," when I know what's going on underneath my own surface thoughts.

Two, being stumped by my own "stuff" makes me a much better therapist because I know what it's like to be held captive by my own limited thinking. And I know what it is like to be released from that thinking and feel the lightness inside. I know what it is like to laugh after a breakthrough – when I feel the relief from a belief that, a few moments earlier, had been a source of deep pain, humiliation, embarrassment, or anger to me. I know the process of transformation, inside and out. I know how to lead people through the process of recognizing their subconscious limiting beliefs and then releasing them.

Using hypnosis, I take people back to the root cause of their limiting beliefs. Our subconscious mind holds all of our beliefs, locked in time at the moment they were formed. It's as though they froze in that moment in our brain. In sessions, once I help my clients go back to the root belief (the cause of their being stuck), then I use a simple process to bring their thinking up to current time where they can then release the untrue belief. I always begin with the client's "original child thoughts and experiences," then release their hold on the adult.

I've worked with thousands and thousands of people over the past 35 years and have seen the quality of their lives change as they shifted their perceptions about themselves, others, events that have happened to them, and life in general. Even after all these years, I still consider it a true miracle when I witness a person release the thinking, emotions and energy that have been causing them suffering and grief, limiting the life they have wanted. One moment they're caught up in the false perception. The next moment they're free of it and life is fundamentally different.

This book is written from my healing journey, the work of my clients, and the wisdom of other authors. I'm not a scientist, so this is not about research and data. This is from my personal experiences with clients changing their lives by changing their limiting beliefs.

THIS BOOK, IN BRIEF

This book has four parts, following this introductory chapter:

- Part I describes the basics: what a belief system is, how it's formed, how to recognize it, and how common limiting beliefs rule your life.

- Part II is about how to change your viewpoint, your story, and your mind so that you can change your future.

- Part III changes perspective and talks from the Soul's viewpoint, describing how your limiting beliefs, which feel like such obstacles, are actually gateways in your Soul's journey, your life lessons, and your purpose in being here. It includes five spiritual qualities that are pathways to your life lessons.

- Part IV is an appendix that lists a number of resources and approaches that can help you change your limiting beliefs and create the future you envision.

But first, it's important to understand why your life is the way it is. Here are a few definitions related to this area of personal growth.

I use some terms interchangeably, although they have somewhat different meanings. **Belief system** is a term I learned years ago, so I use it most often. I will also use the following terms as synonyms: perception, a pattern of behavior, thoughts/feelings, and thoughts infused with energy and emotion.

Dr. Joe Dispenza, in his book *You Are the Placebo*, explains these terms in a different way. On page 164, figure 7.1, he writes:

> "Your thoughts and feelings come from your past memories. If you think and feel a certain way, you begin to create an attitude. Attitudes are shortened states of being. If you string a series of attitudes together, you create a belief. Beliefs are more elongated states of being and tend to become subconscious. When you add beliefs together, you create a perception. Your perceptions have everything to do with the choices you make, the behaviors you exhibit, the relationships you choose, and the realities you create."

WHAT'S THE FINAL GOAL?

I hope this book will trigger memories that unearth your limiting beliefs, which you can then change. My goal is for you to get unstuck from your limiting beliefs, uncover and learn your life lessons, take different actions moving forward, and improve the quality of your life.

I include short client examples because I find them powerful in two ways. One, you may see yourself in a story. Or, two, a story may trigger an out-of-the-blue memory that you come to realize underlies some of your unwanted actions.

In either case, you may have an *aha* insight and, in that moment, you can release the old belief that has been limiting you, nagging you, for years. Of the many ways to change subconscious beliefs, the easiest is the *aha* moment. You have a flash of insight, see the truth of why you're acting and feeling the way you are, and you just let it go. You're free in a matter of seconds. I know this is possible, so I hope it happens for you. I also know that some beliefs are far more stubborn. They take more work. But that's what this book is about: How your limiting beliefs became entrenched in your subconscious mind....and how to update them to empowering beliefs.

I begin by focusing on how limiting beliefs form and engrain themselves in our lives. Many books only say that's what happens in childhood. They don't explain the various ways this happens. There are so many misconceptions about how beliefs form. My clients are always, always amazed at how their limiting thinking began. By spending time exploring a belief, you can see the reason behind your underlying thinking, and why this reason is no longer valid.

Some schools of thought say: "Simply focus on what you want." "Where your attention goes, energy flows." "Don't worry about the past." "Just think positive thoughts." Such lines of reasoning focus on "the law of attraction," where you put all of your energy and attention on your visions and dreams. While this approach has great merit and truth, for some people, past wounds are just too hurtful to get beyond. Their early programming is so strong that it keeps them in that past muck and mire. They can't think or envision their way out of their lack-and-limitation mentality.

As with all of life, balance is needed. Putting all of one's energy and attention into the past is no healthier than ignoring it completely or trying relentlessly to pull that "baggage" along with you as you think positive thoughts and plan your dream life. I believe that both looking back and looking forward are needed for an abundant life. There is work to be done in releasing past limiting programming. But that doesn't create your future. You also need to vision, dream, and take action steps towards your heart's desires.

My final goal for you is to improve the quality of your life by changing your limiting thinking patterns into thoughts and actions that bring you a life of health, well-being, vitality, abundance, love, happiness, success, fulfillment, and whatever else you desire. This is about becoming the best *you*, and achieving what you set out to learn and become this lifetime.

HOW CHANGE LOOKS IN REAL LIFE

Changing a habit or behavior can occur gradually as you release the underlying emotions or trauma that created the behavior. This change can be like turning down a dimmer switch. You are dimming your undesired behavior – gradually decreasing its frequency and intensity.

A client of mine stuttered since she was five years old. For 35 years she had tried everything she knew to overcome or manage her stuttering. She described it as "exhausting to overcome it." The very act of talking was stressful because, if she knew she would block on an upcoming word, she would quickly choose another way of expressing her thoughts. She could feel the block coming, so anytime she spoke, she was always on "high alert".

She was a happy child who sang, recited poetry, and read stories out loud. That all changed in an instant. One day, she became very afraid as a big dog chased her, running home to her mother. She was so upset that she couldn't get the words out, stuttering as she was trying to tell her mother she was chased. That trauma "stuck" in her mind, as did the stuttering. At age 7, a second pivotal moment occurred that locked in her stuttering: She became frustrated as the speech therapist worked with her with flash cards, objects, toys, and letters, saying to herself, "She's teaching me how to speak and it's not working. This isn't going to change. This person isn't going to help me. It's here and it's never going away!"

As an adult she attended speech workshops and therapies, all to no avail. She was taught that, according to medical science, stuttering couldn't be cured; it can only be managed. Yet she longed for release from this condition that caused her such stress, anxiety, and embarrassment.

During my first session with her, we went back to the incident with the dog and released that energy. We also worked with her belief "it's here and it's never going away."

For the following four or five days, she was very relaxed as she spoke and she experienced no stuttering! But then, the old habits came back and she returned to her previous habit of blocking words. Even though she had been free of stuttering for several days, her fears that "it can't be gone. It's can't be that easy!" brought back the habit.

So in our second session, we worked on releasing her fears that "it isn't going to change" and "my speech will never flow." We didn't need to work on the stuttering, because that wasn't really the problem any more. Her doubts and fears were the issue.

After that session, she experienced even more change than after the first session. For a couple of weeks she experienced peace and calm when she was talking, not even thinking about it. It was easy to talk for the first time in 35 years. But then the old habits began to creep back in during everyday stresses. When she felt herself rushing, her speech became affected.

So we did a third session, again going back to the 5-year-old being chased by the dog. The stuttering began as a result of her rushing and high anxiety, and those were the same conditions bringing the stuttering back again. So we worked on releasing her reactions to those two conditions, and we also worked on her fear that the stuttering couldn't really go away.

She then had a new insight: At age 7, her speech therapist had told her, "It's not your fault, and there is nothing you can do about it." Knowing it was not her fault that she stuttered had made her feel better because that meant she was not guilty of causing her parents so much trouble. There was nothing she could do about it. But that limiting belief was now holding her back. So we worked to release it.

With her release of all these beliefs and emotions, she has been able to enjoy speaking without effort or blocking or anxiety. In all, this releasing process took five hours over the course of two months' time.

As each shift occurred within her, deeper doubts and fears arose to her conscious mind, where she could then voice them and release them. That's quite typical of how healing occurs. There are deeper layers of limiting beliefs and fears that rise up to the surface until they have all arisen, and the habit or behavior transforms or is released.

This is what it means to improve the quality of your life. You have a vision or goal of what you want and you have limiting beliefs holding you back from that desired outcome. This is what this book is about. So let's get to work.

In short, my purpose in writing this book is two-fold:

For myself: *To deeply connect with my authentic nature and clearly relay my truth, wisdom, and experience of the nature of limiting beliefs and the Soul's journey.*

For you, my reader: *To understand the origin and effects of your limiting beliefs, your Soul's perspective and purpose of those beliefs, and how to move beyond them into a better quality of life.*

EMPOWERING THOUGHTS

- A miracle is a shift in perception.

- These obstacles are often of our own making. Literally, we make them up in our minds.

- Our subconscious mind holds all of our beliefs, locked in time at the moment they were formed.

- Of the many ways to change subconscious beliefs, the easiest is the *aha* moment.

- One moment they're caught up in the false perception. The next moment they're free of it and life is fundamentally different.

PART I

Belief Systems

*A belief system is a thought that you think,
feel, believe, and live out as though it is true.*

2

Where Did This Stinkin' Thinkin' Come From?

Zen teacher and author, Cheri Huber, has written the book *How You Do Anything Is How You Do Everything*. Do you believe that's true for you? How you do *anything* is how you do *everything*? I don't believe that it's true 100% of the time, yet I also believe it's true more than we'd like to acknowledge. Our brain is a pattern-repeating machine. We do the same things over and over.

Dr. Joe Dispenza, neuroscientist, chiropractor, expert in the field of mind-body connection, and bestselling author and lecturer, teaches that 95% of our thoughts are habitual. Today's thoughts are not new to you. You thought them yesterday, last week, last year, ten years ago. Bob Proctor, well known for his international work on manifestation and his appearance on the movie and book *The Secret*, by Rhonda Byrne, states that 95% of us don't actually think at all, we just habitually repeat mental activity, which is not really thinking.

For the most part, we're experiencing the same busy mental activity day after day, year after year, and decade after decade. Thus, the patterns in our lives remain the same.

So how do we get out of this sameness when we want to fundamentally change our thoughts and lives? You hear the saying, "the zebra can't change its stripes," and you may think that applies to you, especially if you have been stuck in a pattern you don't like for decades.

But here's the truth: You're not a zebra and your thought patterns are not stripes. They can be changed.

There are ways out of these vicious cycles of doing and thinking the same things over and over and over, ad nauseum. The first way out is *awareness*. You become aware of the patterns. You notice your thoughts. You scrutinize what you're noticing. You become conscious and present to your thoughts and emotions. You pay attention as though you were an observer of your own life.

"I already do that!" you may say. "I've been aware of these patterns for ten years and it hasn't changed anything. I'm still doing the same old thing. I'm still ruled by fear."

If that's where you are right now, I feel for you. I know that place. I've been there. The good news is that much has changed for me recently, as I've achieved deep resolutions in some of my biggest and longest-held stuck beliefs.

My message to you is this: It's not hopeless. You don't need to continue to feel stuck and discouraged, while strongly desiring to change aspects that just aren't working for you. There is a way out of their hold on your life.

Yes, you may notice your thoughts, and know your patterns, and think there's nothing more you can learn about yourself. If you've done a lot of healing or therapy work, I want you to realize something: *There's more to you than you currently see or recognize.* The groove of your habits is deeper than you realize. What's underneath your behaviors is so familiar and so well known to you that you don't even see it. You may even talk about it. You can hear yourself saying a statement about yourself, such as "that never works out for me" or "I can't do anything right" or "that's just how men/women are." You say it, you know it, and yet you may never even think to question it. Your *belief* is "That's just how I am." But that can change because it's just a belief, not the Truth of who you are.

Foundational beliefs – those below the surface that lead to the unwanted patterns and outcomes in one's life – act as though they are hard-wired into our programming. We take them for granted. We believe, "this is who I am" rather than "that's a thought I keep thinking and acting upon." If you do notice these beliefs, and even question them, and still nothing changes, then there's something deeper and even more *obvious* going on for you. Yes, "obvious."

I know this for sure: Our answers are right in front of us, and we can't or won't see them. That can be so frustrating, but we all can move through and beyond our limitations!

FOUR VIEWS OF LIFE

Before learning about belief systems in 1980, I believed that the world happened to me and I was not responsible for what occurred in my life. I hadn't done any therapy, and although I'd been to a couple of encounter groups during college in the early 1970s, I didn't have much understanding or concept of the role I actually played in my own life. I was simply showing up in life, and feeling the effects of whatever happened around me.

*Life happens **to** me.* In short, life was happening *to* me. Living in this mode is living from a low level of awareness. It's all I knew at the time, and it is all many people know today.

*Life happens **by** me.* As you strive to grow in consciousness, to become more aware, you can move into the awareness of life happening *by* you. This is when you begin to know you have an effect on the world through your consciousness, such as creating parking spaces with your intention. There's effort at this level, yes, but you realize you are actually making things happen in your life that you want to happen.

*Life happens **through** me.* When you grow even more aware and allow life to be lived *through* you, you place yourself in the flow of life. You allow the Divine to move through you as you follow your intuition, inner guidance, or knowing. You surrender to what is, which means that you don't fight against life. You learn the difference between moving through obstacles in your path as you move towards your vision versus swimming upstream against the flow of life. You continue to take bold actions toward your dreams and visions, always following your inner guidance as you make adjustments along the way.

It's not always easy to know if you are bumping into obstacles that you are to move through, or if you are being internally guided onto a different path. One way to know is to look within yourself and see if you still have a passion for the goal you're seeking. Ask yourself, "Does accomplishing this goal make me feel alive?" Even with what appear to be obstacles in your path, you will continue to persevere if this goal is coming from your inner Self, your Soul, your heart, or however you describe it. You can tell when life is happening through you because your destination is not a "should" or "have to" do that is driven by external circumstances. Rather, it comes from within you, and you want to keep going because something inside you is guiding you onward.

However, if you lose all passion for your goal, if it feels dry, or requires too much of your energy, then perhaps you are swimming upstream and are not on the path that the Divine is leading you toward.

Sometimes it's the timing that is off. You get a great idea, it feels real and from deep within you, and you think you should accomplish it now. However, Divine timing is not the same as human timing, so perhaps you are just being given an idea that will take time to bring to fruition, and thus you run into obstacles that continue to deter you until the timing is ripe for success.

Life happens as me. At the highest level of awareness, you allow life to live *as* you. This is how the prophets and great teachers lived, such as Jesus and Buddha. They allowed the Divine to fully express in their thoughts, words, and actions. In essence, they chose to live being fully guided by the Divine. This is the level of consciousness that spiritual seekers desire to reach: enlightenment or being fully awake.

You will find that you spiral through the first three ways of being, moving in and out of each of them at various times and in differing circumstances. As you move along your spiritual path, you will find yourself more often in the "living life through me" phase. Once in a while, you may move into the highest level of awareness. This, however, is not likely to be where you reside full time.

During a weekend workshop on belief systems in 1980, I learned that I am responsible for my thoughts and feelings, and that these thoughts and feelings actually have an impact on my outer world. It took me a long time to come to terms with "responsibility" – that is, how I perceive the world actually starts inside me, not outside of me. I didn't know it then, but I had a lot of work ahead of me.

WHAT IS A BELIEF SYSTEM?

So what is a belief system? First and foremost, a belief system is a thought. It's a thought you think over and over and over, and you experience it as true. You are convinced this thinking is a true representation of the world because you see the effects in your life. It's a thought that has joined with energy, emotions, and feelings. You live it daily. You see it reflected back to you. A belief system is a whole way of being that feels very true because you can point to examples of supporting experiences in your life. It *feels* true to you and therefore it *is* true for you.

For example, here are a few common beliefs: "I am loved," "I need to please others in order to feel loved," "Life is a struggle," "I always have enough of all that I need," "There's not enough money," "The world is a safe place to be," "I don't like stringy or lumpy food," "I'm alone and have to look after myself."

Most *core* beliefs – that is, beliefs that underpin our decisions – start early in our childhood, very often before age six. Beliefs can even start in the womb, but more typically they begin with birth onward. I have found that the pivotal limiting beliefs in life are often formed by age four.

What we're doing as an infant and young child is trying to figure out how to live, how to survive. We are first and foremost learning (1) how to stay safe and (2) how to get love and approval. These are pivotal to our survival because without enough safety *and* love, we will die. So our early beliefs are most concerned with both.

Belief systems help us understand and make sense of life. Think of them as strongly held opinions that determine how we perceive life. In the same way that a computer is programmed, and will only perform according to its programming, so too will we only "perform" according to our programming. We store these beliefs in our subconscious mind. They may be hidden from our conscious awareness, and are often very different from our logical and conscious thoughts about ourselves.

A subconscious belief system forms when an event happens and we decide: "This is how I am." or "This is how life is." Let's say you're six years old, sitting in your first grade class and the teacher asks a question. You raise your hand, proud that you know the answer...but you're wrong! What happens? The other kids may laugh, the teacher may make a comment or give you a look that you perceive as negative, and you freeze in that moment. Time stands still for you as you experience the sensations of humiliation, embarrassment, and stupidity flowing through you. At the same time, you are likely to have some strong thoughts: "I'm so

21

stupid!" or "I'll do anything to never be embarrassed like this again!" or "I need to be sure I'm always right!"

As you freeze in that brief moment in time, a belief system is formed and programmed into your subconscious mind. This belief system has several components that link together as one:

- Your age,

- The event,

- Your emotions,

- Your physical sensations, and

- The thought – your opinion about yourself or the situation.

Once linked, they are wrapped in your consciousness with: "This is TRUTH!" It feels so true in that moment, and this feeling of truth becomes part of that new belief system. So when you have the thought, "I'm so stupid!" it feels true to you in that moment, and so you begin to believe it IS true. It goes from a momentary feeling of a six-year-old to a lifetime of believing it is true about you.

Once these linked elements are written into your subconscious, they become "law." You have determined (1) an aspect of who you are, and (2) how you show up in life. This belief system then begins to define how you feel about yourself (stupid), how you need to be (always right), and what to avoid (anything you say that could embarrass you).

Our actions, thoughts, feelings, and even our physical health, are influenced by these subconscious beliefs. If you have a belief that you are not good enough, then no matter what the reality is, you'll filter your experience through this belief system and feel not good enough. In addition, this thought is like a magnet, drawing situations into your daily life that reinforce and "prove" you're not good enough. The actual truth doesn't matter. Acknowledgement from others isn't believed. You're always concluding: *I'm not good enough.*

In 2005 Dr. Bruce Lipton, a stem cell biologist and university professor, published his first bestselling book, *The Biology of Belief.* He explains epigenetics and scientifically shows how our beliefs play a pivotal role in the creation of our health. This "New Biology" has turned the old science paradigm of "we are the victims of our genetics" on its head. He writes: *"Beliefs control biology!"* His books are well worth reading to gain an easy-to-understand scientific perspective of the roles cells play in the mind-body connection.

In writing this book, my sister Barbara, who is the editor, reminded me of how I linked fainting to dentists and then to all medical procedures. When I was in fourth grade, my class was practicing singing for a performance we were to put on for the other classes. Apparently, I was singing off-key because the teacher (I still remember her name) pointed at me and told me to just "mouth the words." In other words, quit singing out loud. I don't know if the room was stuffy, or if we had been standing a long time, or if the embarrassment traumatized me. But the next thing I knew, I fainted. I had to be carried to the nurse's office and my mother had to come and get me. By then, of course, I was fine. As it so happened, I had a dental appointment that afternoon and my mother thought I was faking my faint to get out of going to the dentist. So it was a double whammy against me that day: I fainted and I had to go to the dentist.

Two years later in sixth grade, I was a helper for the visiting mobile dentist. I would bring the little kids into his trailer that was fully outfitted for his dentistry. It was rather hot and stuffy inside the trailer. I'll never forget that moment when he extracted a tooth from a child and held up the bloody tooth for me to see. Something happened inside me. I immediately got queasy and fainted! That was the end of my helper role.

But more than that, I then began to faint every time I went to the dentist. Then, fainting linked to other medical procedures, such as when a doctor was examining my hurt toe and used medical terminology. I passed out completely, having no idea what happened. For decades I fainted with all shots and needles, as well as at the sight of blood. I have nearly fainted many times when others have told me stories about their surgeries. That one early incident linked to many other medical procedures throughout many years of my life. I learned to always warn the medical staff, "I'm a fainter."

A clear signpost of a belief system is: *this is just how I am, how life is, how it's always been, and how it's supposed to be. It just is.*

Here are five ways to uncover your limiting belief systems:

- Look for patterns in your life

- Notice when you feel childish

- Identify when you react rather than respond

- Be aware of what irritates you

- Pay attention to feedback from others

Let's explore how to be a belief-system detective for yourself.

LOOK FOR PATTERNS IN YOUR LIFE

A powerful way to uncover your belief systems is to look for patterns in your life, which means the same thing keeps happening over and over – and you're sick of it. These patterns can be quite obvious or rather subtle. For instance, if you've always dated the same type of woman, then it's rather easy to spot your underlying beliefs. For you, the woman you're attracted to has to have certain qualities, and those are …. (Fill in the blanks with the similar qualities of all the women you've dated or married.)

Don't put down what you intellectually want. Write down the qualities the women actually have had. It's not just coincidence that they have similarities. It's based on your beliefs, and those beliefs determine whom you attract into your life.

Let's look at a possible pattern. Say you keep attracting women who are resentful of you. Perhaps one was resentful of your money, another of your lack of enough success or ambition, another of simply the fact that you're a man, and so on. You may then go to great lengths to be sure the new woman you just met does not have "the resentment factor." If you find nothing there, you presume she's different. But, six months or two years down the road, bam – there it is! You get into an argument and her festering resentment roars to the surface. You never saw it coming. You were sure it wasn't there. You tried so hard to avoid it. Yet, there it is.

Or, as a woman, perhaps you believe men are narcissistic. Their bottom line is that they care first and foremost about themselves, but, at times, they can make it appear as though they are putting you first. What may confuse you, however, is that you have brothers or male friends who are *not* like that, or male bosses or colleagues who are very kind and considerate of you. However, in one area of your life – your intimate relationships – you keep attracting men who put themselves first – way out in front. And here's the distressing part: You keep on dating them (or marrying them) even when you can see that behavior on the first date! You make excuses for it, rationalize it, just plain ignore it, or not even notice the behavior. That's called denial.

This doesn't make logical sense, but your logical mind is *not* in charge here. Your subconscious belief – "this is how men are" – rules here. When you trigger a belief, especially in relationships, your adult sensibilities go to sleep and your early child experiences take over. So your three-year-old is determining whom you are involved with, based on your early family perceptions and experiences.

Needless to say, this isn't a very good system for creating healthy, long-lasting intimate relationships. Understanding this helps explain why so many relationships don't work out, doesn't it?

NOTICE WHEN YOU FEEL CHILDISH

Another way to spot when you are in the throes of a limiting belief is when you feel younger than you are, like a child, or overwhelmed by something that an adult should be able to do. The situation can feel too much, or too big, or too confusing. You have the feeling "This doesn't make any sense! I'm an adult, but I can't do this for some reason."

Here's an example. Years ago, I worked with an intelligent, educated woman who wanted to invest in the stock market. But whenever she looked at the financial pages, all the numbers swam in front of her eyes. She couldn't focus or understand the information. She even dated stockbrokers and took classes in investing, but she just couldn't make sense of all that data.

Using hypnosis I helped take her back to the origin of this limiting belief system. She discovered that her underlying belief started when she was five and overwhelmed by kindergarten. As a child learning something new, she had an overwhelming sensation of "This is too much for me." That sensation was replayed every time she opened the financial pages. Her brain would trigger the original event and she would again become five years old. A five-year-old typically can't understand the symbols and numbers on a financial page. Even though her 35-year-old self wanted the information – and she was fully capable of understanding it and making good decisions – she would feel "This is too much for me." It made no sense to her at all until she uncovered the original belief and was able to release her childish thinking and update it to her adult-self reading the financial pages and investing.

Or take another example. Imagine *you* are a three-year-old in the throes of panic and fear because your Mommy has just left you. Suddenly, you cannot tell yourself, "I'm fine." While you're caught in this fear, that's your reality; so these are the feelings through which you filter your experience. When something happens to change your experience, such as being comforted by a loving and caring person who says, "Mommy will be home soon; she's just gone to work," then your consciousness will change, dissipating your panic and fear – and you calm down.

Now imagining yourself thirty years later and you're in a relationship in which your love threatens to leave you, or actually does leave you. Your brain immediately scans to find what it knows about a loved one leaving you, which triggers the memory of your childhood experience. As this memory is activated and replayed, you experience the panic and fear in the same way, and often with the same intensity, as you did at age three. And, as that original panic and fear replays in your mind and body, it feels absolutely real to you. You're in the midst of it and believe it to be your reality as the adult.

I can't say often enough: *When a subconscious belief system is activated, you are in the consciousness that created it. It's impossible to solve a problem from that consciousness.*

But, just because you're experiencing the panic and fear doesn't mean it's accurate or real. But while in that emotional state, you are convinced it is legitimate and accurate. The "this is true" consciousness is the same as when Mommy left you. You feel young and panicked – again.

When you're caught in a strong emotion, you may justify that it's appropriate or there's nothing you can do about it, thinking, "that's just the way I am," or "anyone would feel this way!" In this consciousness, nothing will change. You will continue to replay the original beliefs and continue to experience heartbreak as people leave you.

IDENTIFY WHEN YOU REACT RATHER THAN RESPOND

This is similar to the previous way of discovering your belief systems because when you respond to a situation, you come from your adult beliefs, behaviors and thinking. You have a range of possibilities in how you respond and the freedom to change your mind. On the other hand, when you react negatively to another person's language, actions, or even a look, your reaction is coming from your childhood thinking. When another person triggers you, there you go, sliding down a slippery emotional slope into negativity, anger, fear, disgust, judgment, righteousness, or a myriad of other disempowering emotions. Your mind starts going a mile a minute with all sorts of negative thoughts. It's as though you have no control over your reaction.

Let's say that you are in a meeting or gathering with numerous others, and there is a person with whom you have "issues." Basically, you have judgments or resentments about him and see him as "holier than thou" and a show off. As he shares his opinion and ideas, you begin to experience old familiar thoughts and feelings moving through your mind and body. You begin to have an internal dialogue, such as, "Who does he think he is, Mr. High and Mighty? Anyone can see that's a dumb idea. Why does he have to talk so much? I just wish he'd shut up and let others have a say. He doesn't know what he's talking about." All the time you're having this internal dialogue with yourself, you're getting more and more agitated and annoyed. And there seems to be nothing you can do to stop it. It's as though you're on a runaway train and there's no stopping it. You have hopped onto this track and it's taking you away from your adult self.

The thing is, this isn't the first time you've had this same reaction. This is all very familiar to you. It may be a different person and different details, but it's the same basic reaction you have to anyone you consider to be a show off.

When this happens, you are not coming from the consciousness of your adult thinking; rather, you are replaying a scenario from childhood that happened many years ago. You can identify that you are reacting because you are unable to stop the loop of your judgmental thoughts. If you cannot stop to take a breath, calm your agitation, and listen with an open mind, then you are reacting rather than responding. This means that an incident that occurred thirty, forty or fifty years ago is still actively running your life.

BE AWARE OF WHAT IRRITATES YOU

Do you get irritated by other people driving too fast or, in your opinion, they drive recklessly or aren't paying enough attention to the road? Perhaps it is your spouse or partner whose driving is a constant source of annoyance. If you follow your thinking back to your younger years, I'm sure you will come upon a memory of a time when fast or reckless driving played a role in your life. It could have been your father complaining about other drivers, or your mother commenting on what a terrible driver your father was, or a reckless driver causing an accident that made an impact on you. If others' driving causes you ongoing irritation, then there is a belief inside your mind regarding that behavior. Chances are, that belief formed in your childhood.

For a moment, choose a behavior others have that really irritates or annoys you. Think about the way it makes you feel when you witness it in others. Notice what happens in your mind and your body. Do you start to feel irritated, annoyed, or angry? Do you notice your heart starting to beat faster or your stomach clenching? Your physical reaction is a clue to let you know the judgment you have is not based in your adult thinking. Rather, it's from earlier in life. If it were from current adult thinking, you could be neutral and see it as "just what is" without emotional or mental anguish. Your irritability is a signal that you have emotions and judgments all wound together regarding a behavior that, most likely, you also have in some respect.

PAY ATTENTION TO FEEDBACK
FROM OTHERS

Have you ever noticed others talk or complain about a trait of yours? Rather than close your ears or defend yourself, listen up! They're providing you great feedback about your behavior (which is you acting out one of your limiting beliefs). Or, viewed another way, do your relationships often end for the same reason? For example, do your partners tell you, "You're not really emotionally present for me?" When you receive such negative feedback from, friends, family, partners, and co-workers, wake up! They're pointing out a limiting belief.

This approach to uncovering your limiting beliefs doesn't take deep analysis. In your everyday life, it appears right in front of you – from feedback, from your thinking, from your behaviors, and from your results. In fact, all of life is giving you continual feedback on your beliefs, including both beliefs that serve and uplift you and those that keep you from the quality of life you desire.

BELIEFS ARE IN PLAIN SIGHT

All five ways of uncovering our belief systems can occur in a short span of time and are usually right in front of us, even if we can't see them. Here's my personal experience with all five intertwined, which is how life usually plays out.

I woke up on a Monday morning, February 17, 2014, with a very sore right neck and shoulder. I thought, "That's strange. I must have slept wrong. It'll be fine in a couple of days." Then I pretty much ignored it because I had already determined its cause: sleeping wrong. Yet, the pain persisted and was excruciating.

As "luck" would have it, I had a brief planning session that day with Jon Robson, www.meta-medicineusa.com, a talented

Transformational Health Practitioner in Colorado. He's a master trainer of META-Medicine® and is skilled in the work of Dr. John Demartini on transforming one's thinking. (There's much more about this in later chapters).

Jon and I were examining my beliefs and patterns that were keeping me from writing. At the time, I had been in California for three weeks and hadn't yet begun to write. I mentioned to him my sore neck and shoulder and he told me that they represented a mind-body connection: "They're about moral dilemmas and judgment." Oh, yes, that rang a bell. I was fearful of writing wrong information or having a reader misinterpret or misuse my words, to their detriment. It's never my intention to cause harm, so that fear was holding me captive.

Three days later, I had an extended session with Jon and it was extraordinary, to say the least. I felt shifts occurring on a very deep level. I knew something inside had changed. But, still I resisted writing. In fact, my neck and shoulder hurt more, and I didn't want to even *think* of writing.

This is typical of a healing journey: It's not all up, up, up. But downs, as well as ups, are also good news because they mean you're on the path, stirring up the hornets' nest inside you. Your body's resistance is up, causing physical sensations, and so are all its signals that you're meant to follow.

I did another session the following week, working more directly on my various fears of being judged by you, my reader, and feeling responsible for how you might use my information. Intellectually, I knew better than that. But deep inside, I could not shake my judgment. That's how beliefs are. When thinking as an adult, we know better. But our child's thinking wins out time and again.

And then, all of a sudden, I changed inside.

I woke up the next morning and worked on this book for three hours. That, in itself, was a miracle. In the past year, I could never write for more than one hour, because it made me feel like I was going crazy inside. That morning, though, to my surprise and delight, I also found that I had actually written much more in the preceding year than I had realized.

The following morning, I spent another two hours pulling it all together and discovered I already had 20,000 words. That amazed me!

That's how it works when you release limiting beliefs and fears. Your life changes in real and measurable ways. You simply act, feel, and think differently. As a result, you realize that what you need already exists, and has all along. You just couldn't see it or think of it because the filters of your limiting beliefs blocked you.

And yet … my neck and shoulder continued to hurt. The pain was less, but definitely not gone. Writing didn't make it go away, and neither did a visit to the chiropractor. I expected that the pain "should" have gone away as I released the energy and emotions of my underlying beliefs. Alas, no.

But rather than search for deeper underlying causes, I did what I've always done with symptoms that annoyed me (in other words, I followed my subconscious beliefs): I ignored them. I intuitively knew there wasn't anything structurally or seriously wrong and western medicine couldn't do anything for me. I continued to believe it had something to do with writing. That's as far as I could get in my self-diagnosis.

I wrote most mornings for several hours, and enjoyed the process. I thought this routine would take care of the pain by showing myself that doing what I felt was necessary. I was doing enough.

I'm explaining this in detail so that you can see the ways in which you might have a similar experience. You try one thing and it helps some, and then another, and another, with some progress. All the while your beliefs are playing out in your life. Then you think, "I just have to live with this until it goes away on its own. I've done all I know how to do. Nothing is working. I can put up with this. It's good enough."

These words, "I can put up with this," keep us stuck. Meanwhile, inside, something urges us on. "What's next?" There's a saying: "Good is the enemy of great." I was willing to settle for "good" (some pain) rather than going for "great" (no pain).

It's wonderful to have friends who don't let you get away with ignoring obvious problems. I have several in my life who call me on my "stuff." I'm ever grateful, even in the moment when I'm not really pleased.

A good friend and colleague, Dr. Kim Jobst, also a friend of Jon Robson (two fabulous Brits), is a highly trained master and "wizard" in the field of mind-body-soul connection. In addition to being a physician and homeopath, he's the editor-in-chief of the *Journal of Alternative and Complementary Medicine*. He also teaches and writes on the meanings of diseases, and diseases of meaning. He's an expert and genius in this field. It's what he does and knows. He wouldn't let me off the hook.

"What is your shoulder saying to you?" he asked me. "How is it trying to help?" Simple questions. I even ask them of others in similar situations. But I couldn't come up with answers. My mind wandered all over the place, but couldn't pinpoint my issue, my belief. I was tired and grumpy. I wanted to stop talking about my pain; yet he persisted.

Here's something I'd like you to realize, pay attention to, and really sit with for yourself: If you have an issue that won't go away – regardless of how many weeks, months, years or decades you've worked on it – no matter how much grief, heartache, and destruction it has caused you, it's *not* against you. Originally, the underlying belief was meant *for* your highest good. The more it resists changing, the more important it *was* for you when you took it on.

That seems so contradictory and downright wrong, doesn't it? On the physical human side, it doesn't make much sense. The disease is killing you, your saboteur is destroying your finances, you keep picking absolutely wrong partners, or you can't lose weight and keep it off – no matter what you do.

However, on your Soul level – that is, the aspect of you that *really* matters – resolving these issues that resist change is important work. Your body is trying to get your attention because there's something underneath that you're not seeing or listening to. Actually, you may know *exactly* what your body is telling you and you choose to ignore it. Or you may have inklings or a sense of it, but can't quite stare it in the face to discern the truth within or stare it down into submission.

I believe we usually know, deep down, but our old habits and fears quickly rise up and stamp back our knowing. And so the pain, addiction, old habits, and lifelong self-sabotaging patterns continue.

After talking a while with Kim via Skype, I wanted to quit or change the subject. "It doesn't really matter that much," I thought, "and this talking isn't working…" I was irritated with myself for not being able to get answers. My thoughts were: "I feel like a 'bad' client; I can't do this right now; it's late; and (best of all) I'm wasting his time." I wished I could disconnect Skype. Does this line of rationalizing feel familiar to you? Our minds get so resistant in order to push us back from facing and changing our old beliefs.

And then, he hit one of my "hidden-in-plain-sight truths." He said, "You're not writing from your heart." I had been writing in my familiar way, "doing what I've always done, it's how I am." I was writing from my knowledge and experience, that is, from my head, from my logical mind. It was good information, and it's what I want to bring to the world. I love this subject!

But, my heart wanted to have a voice. My Soul wanted me to also write from my heart, not just from my knowledge. I intuitively recognized that I hadn't been putting my heart into my writing. I wasn't feeling love coming through me as I wrote. What I had written felt sterile and I had responded by telling myself "I'll come back later and liven it up."

I'd had the sense that something was wrong, but I couldn't find the right words to describe my unsettling feeling – until then.

From that opening, I realized my issue on its deeper and broader level: Opening my heart is what I've come to learn and express this lifetime. How do I live from my heart, be more intimate, and not just live from my head? I'm not talking about just romantic intimacy, but heart-centered connection as a way of being.

Since knowing this is one of my main life lessons, I've made conscious choices to keep coming more from my heart rather than just my head. It's a long process for all of us. If you have this same learning, you may think it's less painful, safer actually, to live from your intellect. That's how I was raised. "Use your noodle (mind)," our father would say to each of us, and tap our head. There wasn't deep emotional connection in my family, so it wasn't something I knew much about. "Lead with your head, your knowledge. That's how you make it in the world," was the belief I took on. We kids didn't realize how much Dad actually used his intuition because we only heard about using our mind.

So, as I was writing this book, I instinctively led with my head. I'd keep asking myself, "What do I know about this subject?" It's not bad or wrong to use our logical mind. We absolutely need it. But should it always be our default mode? Is that where you go for safety, too?

EMPOWERING THOUGHTS

- You're not a zebra and your thought patterns are not stripes. They can be changed.

- A belief system is a whole way of being that feels very true.

- A clear signpost of a belief system is: *this is just how I am, how life is, how it's always been, and how it's supposed to be. It just is.*

- When a subconscious belief system is activated, you are in the consciousness that created it. It's impossible to solve a problem from that consciousness.

- You can identify that you are reacting because you are unable to stop the loop of your judgmental thoughts.

- Originally, the underlying belief was meant *for* your highest good.

3

Characteristics of Beliefs

Now that you are aware of five easy ways to spot "stinkin' thinkin'" – look for patterns in your life, notice when you feel childish, identify when you react rather than respond, be aware of what irritates you, and listen to feedback from others – let's look at eight characteristics of both limiting and empowering beliefs:

- Beliefs form in a moment in time

- Beliefs grow stronger over time

- Beliefs often aren't logical

- Beliefs act as magnets

- We don't always create our own reality...

- ...Sometimes our Soul creates our reality

- Beliefs also form in adulthood

- When tragedy strikes, re-evaluate your life

BELIEFS FORM IN A MOMENT IN TIME

As children and adults, we are always forming beliefs from our everyday experiences. Most support us; some limit us. Our limiting beliefs are not always, or even typically, formed from traumatic, abusive events. In fact, a limiting belief can be formed from a positive experience.

As an example, in one of my classes, a woman in her 60s asked why she always needed to get approval from a man to feel good about herself.

During a short exercise in the class using mild-trance hypnosis, I gave the suggestion to go back to the root cause of a limiting pattern. That simple suggestion, combined with the relaxation that gives access to our subconscious mind, "automatically" takes us back to the origination of the belief we hold in our mind.

This woman went back to being five years old. Her father was standing with his arm around her shoulders, bragging to the neighbor about how proud he was of his little girl. That feeling of love and pride swept through her, and in that moment she formed the belief "this is how I feel good about myself." In that moment, that was absolutely the truth for her. She was being loved and acknowledged by her father and the neighbor. It felt good, as it should have. That was good fatherly parenting.

Unfortunately, rather than just being a good moment in her life, that belief got stuck in her thinking and became generalized to the rest of her life as a rule: "this is how I feel good about myself. I get approval from a man."

Many beliefs are formed from an event that happens in the blink of an eye. In fact, we can form one when someone gives us a dirty look. Perhaps it's "the look" from a parent that you learn means that you're in trouble. You translate that look to mean, "I'm not loved," or "I'm not good enough," or "I need to be very, *very* careful in life."

I worked with one client for over a year as she moved through many of her limiting beliefs on poor self-esteem. When she got down to a core event that had given rise to so much of her lack of self worth, it was a simple event, not a big trauma. She was at school, 6 or 7 years old, and went to sit down on a bench. It was a small bench, only room for a couple of kids. There was a popular girl sitting on the bench who said to her, "No, you can't sit here!"

In that moment, with the look and the inflection of that girl's words, my client took in all that disapproval and made it mean many things to her: She wasn't good enough, not pretty enough, not popular enough, and simply and completely, not enough. Such a simple little event, and yet it created the thinking that crippled her ability to feel good about herself for decades.

BELIEFS GROW STRONGER OVER TIME

Think of a belief as a little pathway in your brain when it's first formed. There's not much to it. It's barely there. But, when a certain belief is reinforced – either by being told you're not good enough or experiencing it for yourself – it's as though you're walking on that path, making it more definitive – turning it into a rut. Over time, this rut becomes wider and deeper, going from a path to a road. And then it begins to have roads link off of it, as other beliefs become connected. Later with more experiencing and reinforcing of that belief, it becomes a major thoroughfare.

41

If you continue to experience a belief, such as "I'm not good enough," as true for you, and you reinforce it by perceiving yourself in more and more areas as not good enough, it eventually becomes a super-highway with all sorts of roads and highways leading off it. Your thinking automatically goes there because it's such a firmly established thought process within you. It becomes your default self-concept. You've experienced it often enough and with enough emotion that you are convinced it's true. The thought "I'm not good enough" that began as a young child becomes insidious and takes over your adult view of yourself in the world.

BELIEFS OFTEN AREN'T LOGICAL

In many ways, it makes no sense why one simple event can create a belief that is taken in so deeply and has such a long-lasting and destructive influence, while other traumatic events don't have the same outcome.

Unfortunately, there doesn't seem to be any rhyme or reason for the beliefs caused by different events. You often can't figure them out because beliefs aren't formed using logic. They're formed by perceptions – of the child or young person – and programmed into the subconscious. They made sense to the child in the moment they were formed, but they don't make sense to the adult.

Have you ever noticed how differently siblings can view their childhood and their upbringing? Each can provide very different descriptions of their family's life. It can seem as though they were raised in different households by different parents. Why? Siblings have their own perceptions of their family life. Their relationships with their parents and other siblings differ because they each developed their own belief systems, which were then reinforced through their different life experiences.

I worked with two sisters regarding the same event in which they developed opposing beliefs. As young girls, they were riding home in the back seat of the car, having enjoyed a family day of fun at a carnival. As they rode, the girls began to ask for something to drink because they were thirsty. Their father turned around, pointed his finger at them and said, "You girls are never satisfied!"

One of the sisters took that statement in as truth and formed a long-lasting belief about never being satisfied. The other sister told herself, "That's not true," and went on with her ride home.

Years later, when I worked with them, the first sister was indeed living out the belief of never being satisfied: She was overweight (not enough food), not happy with her job, not enough money, and not terribly satisfied in her marriage or husband. It was a theme, an ongoing pattern, in her life.

The other sister had none of these issues. She had a fulfilling job and marriage, enough money to live comfortably, and was basically pretty happy and fulfilled.

At the same moment in time, these two girls moved in opposite directions in their lives – all because of how they responded to one statement from their parent. This is powerful stuff, isn't it? But parents, don't despair. Their father did *not* cause their beliefs. Their *own* perceptions led to their differing results.

I worked with another woman who had been gang raped by five guys she knew. The next day she saw them and was able to look each of them in the face. With that act of confronting each one, she took back her power from that event. I was sure she would have at least a few limiting beliefs from that event, but we couldn't find anything still active in her.

However, a few sessions later, a memory surfaced of a man stepping out of the bushes and flashing her, before he ran off. In this case, she wasn't able to process it with him or in any way create closure. This momentary event did lead her to form destructive and limiting beliefs about herself and her safety around men.

BELIEFS ACT AS MAGNETS

Once our beliefs form, they act as magnets, drawing similar life experiences to us. This is what creates the "self-fulfilling prophesy" of our thinking. It seems to be one of the mysteries of the Universe, and yet it's quite real.

Think of your mind as a radio station broadcasting different songs. Each of your energized beliefs is a different song, with a different frequency or signal. The energy and emotion contained within the belief determines the strength of each belief's signal. When you have a highly energized belief in your subconscious mind (that is, it feels very true to you), you broadcast that signal out into the world where others pick it up with a matching signal. That is, they are tuned into that same belief and are drawn into your life.

The more you focus on your belief, the stronger the signal you send out, and the more you "magnetize" matching experiences into your life. This is especially true when you use such language as, "I never" and "I always." When you think, "I never have enough money," that's the energy and vibration you're sending out... and that's what you then draw into your life – again and again and again.

Whenever I teach this in a class, my students always ask questions about world events and crises, and whether we are responsible for them occurring in our lives.

WE DON'T ALWAYS CREATE
OUR OWN REALITY...

We don't actually create our own reality – meaning, we are *not* in charge of everything that happens to us. That goes too far. Obviously, there are many influencers in life. Yes, our beliefs are strong influencers, but they are not the only ones. Life has mysteries that go beyond our beliefs and beyond our creation.

During the 1980s, the saying, "You create your own reality" was a form of metaphysical malpractice. Anything that happened to you – from a head cold to an accident to a life-threatening disease – was turned back on you as your fault. "Why did you create that?" was a common query.

The truth is that we don't deliberately, or even consciously, draw terrible things to us. Sometimes, life just happens, and we are involved.

...SOMETIMES OUR SOUL
CREATES OUR REALITY

Sometimes our life experiences have nothing whatsoever to do with our beliefs. That's pretty much the opposite of everything I've been describing here, isn't it? But it's true, because sometimes what happens to us, or around us, is part of our Soul's learning for this lifetime. Or sometimes life happens and we're affected.

By living through a trauma, we become stronger. So often an experience that is horrendous on the human level can be a great learning on the Soul level.

Young children who are molested or abused absolutely do not cause those experiences because of their beliefs. They have no concept of that sort of violence or betrayal. Children are always innocent. But from those abusive events, these children form beliefs that direct their thinking and self-concept down a certain pathway. They then may spend many years undoing the harm that was done to them – mentally, emotionally, physically and psychologically.

During this process of healing, these abused people may become stronger, more confident, find their voice, and learn to no longer view themselves as victims. Or, they fall prey to the harm done to them and never escape their victimhood, even passing it on to their children by marrying an abusive partner or being abusive themselves. Whichever pathway they take, their Soul is learning, because it learns from negative as well as positive situations.

BELIEFS ALSO FORM IN ADULTHOOD

Even though I emphasize childhood beliefs, not all limiting beliefs form in childhood. Traumatic events can form new limiting beliefs at any age. The tragedy of the Twin Towers' destruction on 9/11/01 changed many people's beliefs around the world. Those who witnessed that morning may have been forever changed. Until then, they may have always felt safe, and yet, in the blink of an eye, they began to feel unsafe in the world.

Many survivors, as well as friends and relatives of those killed that day, made major changes in their lives. That event may even have put them on their spiritual path, perceiving the fragility or preciousness of life in a whole new way, finding purpose out of the tragedy. Others may have fallen victim to the horror of that day and spiraled downward in their lives.

People who were calm before 9/11 may have begun to experience fears and anxieties. People did stop flying, for a while. Others began to save food or ammunition for defense against an enemy. Others went on with their lives without being affected – other than to feel badly about all those who were harmed. They felt compassion and sympathy, but the event didn't dramatically change their lives. The event was the same but the impact was different for each person. Some dramatically shifted their beliefs about the world, while others reinforced their beliefs about the callousness of mankind.

There was one event and yet each person responded in their own way, through their own perceptions, and changed their beliefs accordingly.

Likewise, recessions can cause people to change their beliefs, or bring up long-buried beliefs. Those who always felt financially stable and secure in their work places and homes could have their security beliefs dramatically challenged during a recession, or from losing a job, or from having their home in foreclosure. Life as they had always known it, and had expected it to continue, was no longer their reality. New beliefs formed, or perhaps beliefs from childhood arose in new and powerful ways. Or perhaps a recession was part of their Soul's journey – to experience the ability to rebound without losing hope. Such events may occur so that these people really look at their lives and honestly evaluate what has and hasn't been working – on a heart-centered level.

WHEN TRAGEDY STRIKES, RE-EVALUATE YOUR LIFE

Personal tragedies are a time to re-evaluate your life. Being laid off from work often causes great stress and losses of many kinds in one's life. Yet, at the same time, it can become the best gift you have ever received because you are being asked to go inside yourself and decide, "What would I really like to do next?" Tragedy can force you to change your thinking and actions in order to create a new life for yourself and your family. How you respond to such situations is entirely your choice.

Please remember this: There are always multiple ways you could respond to your situation. But to embark on the "untaken route," you must step outside your traditional thinking and acting – look through a new lens – to conjure up the wealth of possibilities for your life. Such mental exploration may feel unreal at first, but start anyway.

For example, if you've lost your job, imagine getting paid to do something that you'd love to do for free. There's likely a job that fits your desire and your talent. Envision your new, desired outcome. Test it out. Feel already having it. It might not match your old, habitual lifestyle at all. Yes, this is easier said than done, especially when your life appears to be in chaos and you in confusion. But, you can do it. There are many techniques for changing your thinking. Some of them are listed in Part IV, the Resources section.

Divorce also causes many core limiting and positive beliefs to rise up and become highly charged. You will go through a phase where you look at your relationship through your filters, such as *"I can't do anything right." "I'm a failure." "Men/women can't be trusted." "I'm afraid to be alone." "I don't know what to do."* And so on. These beliefs all feel so very real and true. They are highly charged with all the emotions you're feeling, including anger, disappointment, shock, fear, uncertainty, and betrayal – to name just a few.

When tragedy strikes, it's the time to buckle down and take an inventory of your thinking – and uncover your "stinkin' thinkin'" because it has limited your life. It's time to give it the boot.

Now, we turn to the nitty gritty of beliefs by exploring examples of actual limiting beliefs. Notice if you see yourself in any of the following descriptions.

EMPOWERING THOUGHTS

- Many beliefs are formed from an event that happens in the blink of an eye.

- You often can't figure them out because beliefs aren't formed using logic.

- Once our beliefs form, they act as magnets, drawing similar life experiences to us.

- So often an experience that is horrendous on the human level can be a great learning on the Soul level.

4

Common Limiting Beliefs

Logically speaking, it doesn't make any sense to hold onto limiting beliefs once we've recognized them, does it? If our logical mind were in control of our subconscious beliefs, our life would be very different. We would notice our negative thoughts or unwanted behaviors, determine that's not how we want to be, decide how we want to be, and voila, our life would change. That's how our logical mind would work.

However, our deeply held limiting beliefs are not ruled by our logical mind. While it's very true that most of our subconscious beliefs change and grow with us as we mature, some remain stuck in their original form. Remember this: *most* of our childhood beliefs are updated throughout our life. So most of our beliefs do work for us. Only a minor number cause us grief. Those are the mal-adaptive ones; they remain based on our childhood thinking.

One of the main reasons we hold onto these old beliefs is because, when formed, they were meant to help us. All beliefs are. Originally, we saw each one as a solution to a problem. Since many of our beliefs were formed before age seven, many were based on (1) being loved and accepted and having a sense of belonging, or (2) feeling safe and secure. We all have these core needs, so beliefs tied to them tend to stay intact. In addition, if we formed a belief based on these core needs during a time of high emotion, those emotions continue to act as glue to keep that belief static.

So let's explore some common limiting beliefs, as well as some possible "positive intents" for why we originally formed these beliefs. See which beliefs strike a chord in you – either in a feeling, an emotion, a memory popping up, a shiver up your arms or your spine, a gasp, or the thought, "Oh my gosh, that's me," or "Wow, so that's where my belief came from," or "I don't feel so good right now, those words hurt."

- "I'm not enough"

- "There's something wrong with me"

- "I get abandoned"

- "Why did he (or she) reject me?"

- "I'm afraid"

- "I have to … I should … I can't … I don't want to"

- "I'm stuck"

- "I'm alone … I'm all on my own … I don't belong"

- "I'm afraid to speak up"

- "I don't matter....I'm not worthy"

- "I can't do it right"

- "I need to be in control"

- "I've been abused"

- "Life isn't fair"

- "I'm powerless"

"I'M NOT ENOUGH"

As children, we all learned some aspects of being "not enough." Variations of this belief are: I'm not good enough, not smart enough, not tall enough, not thin enough, not rich enough, not athletic enough, not coordinated enough, not attractive enough, and so on.

By the time you were a few years old, you were probably told by your parents, "No! Bad!" This isn't in any way to blame your parents (or you as the parent). It's just how life is with little children. The problem occurs when, as a young child, you believe it's about you, rather than about your behavior. At a very young age, the feeling begins to form "I'm not good enough for Mommy or Daddy. There's something lacking in me."

At a very early age, most children learn that pleasing Mommy and Daddy and making them happy is what gets children love and keeps them feeling safe. Since love and safety are core needs, these beliefs and perceptions tend to become deeply ingrained in the subconscious.

Imagine you're two years old and acting appropriately for a two-year-old, which may mean your mother is overwhelmed and feeling crazy. She's saying (yelling) you are bad, what you're doing isn't good enough, and you should know better. You may take this in with all the emotion and charged energy of that moment, feeling as though the "I Am" that you are isn't good enough. It's not that your actions are bad. Rather, you believe that, to the very core of you, *You* are bad.

When the *I'm not good enough* shifts from something that you're *doing* to who you *are* as an essence, your sense of self, your sense of worth, diminishes. Your vibrant child-light dims. If this message gets replayed and re-experienced often enough, it can feel as though your inner light gets completely covered over by this sense of "in the very core of my Being, I am not good enough."

I'm not good enough is a lie, just as are all the other limiting beliefs.

It was never the truth, not even for a moment. Your actions as a child that led to being called bad were, most likely, age appropriate. They weren't the actions of an adult; they were the actions of a child. Even if what you did was "bad," no matter what it was (and, think about it, how bad can a little child actually be?), it was always about your behavior and never about You – the core and Soul of who you are. And yet that's what you took it to mean: You, the very core of you, is bad. And that's a lie.

You may also form this belief simply because you are a younger sibling. If you're three years old and your siblings are five or seven or ten, you compare yourself to them. You see that you're simply not at their skill level. Since "age-appropriate abilities" is not a concept you understand, you think you should be able to do whatever they can do. But since you can't do as well as they can do, or keep up with them, then you generalize and tell yourself, *"I'm not as good as them. I can't do it as well as anyone else."*

A belief system not only includes a *thought*, such as *I'm not good enough*, but also accompanying physical sensations, which strengthen the thought's power over you. When that belief is replayed, these sensations rise up: You can feel your body shrink inward, your stomach contract, your head and shoulders hang down, your arms or legs shake, or other bodily reactions.

In addition, a belief system also includes the emotions and feelings we originally experienced in that moment, such as sadness, despondency, hopelessness, and a sense of no worth or value.

And that's not all! A belief system also includes the event and our age when that belief was programmed into our subconscious. All these elements intertwine, connect, and lock together, becoming one big limiting wall – walling us off from achieving our potential. Over time, this limiting wall can become so habitual that it becomes engrained in our body – we don't even realize it is fencing us in.

Here's an example. Let's say you're five years old playing kickball. You mess up and miss the ball. All the other kids laugh and make fun of you. In that moment, you can freeze for an instant and unconsciously record the entire event in your subconscious mind: five years old, humiliated, laughed at, not good enough, feel awful, just can't do anything right, others can do everything better than me. That entire moment in time becomes the basis for the belief system, *I'm not good enough* or *when I try and do something, I get humiliated* or *I'm no good at sports*.

In most cases, such an event is a moment in time and, within a short time, the emotional charge dissipates and the entire event dissolves away, leaving no long-term impact on your life. However, in some cases, such a simple event can get energetically stuck in your mind and become the basis for your self-concept. Over time, it takes on a life of its own, as it becomes the filter for how you see yourself and your place in the world.

From then on, when you make a mistake or a bad decision, or take some wrong action, this belief will get triggered in you – thereby reinforcing and "proving" to yourself that you are, indeed, not good enough. You will look at your life and see the huge pile of "evidence" that others are better than you. You will relive the consciousness of that kickball event thousands of times. And each time, you will feel as you did at age 5 – young and childish.

Why does this "evidence" pile up? Because when a belief is energetically charged, it becomes a magnet for situations with the same energetic charge (*I'm not good enough*) to occur over and over as you age. You literally send out the subconscious thought *"I'm not as good as others and I get humiliated,"* which draws to you circumstances where you perceive yourself as not as good as others. In fact, it may be that you truly aren't doing as well as others, so feeling embarrassed and humiliated seem justifiable. "See, I knew I couldn't do it!" could be your mantra. Over time, it becomes self-perpetuating as it occurs more and more often. It gets so that you then simply expect it to happen.

Most of our beliefs change and grow as we develop and mature. Thoughts and beliefs we had as children fall away naturally and don't cause any sort of stress or problems later on in life.

However, some beliefs do not change or grow. They stay suspended in time, stuck in the moment in which they were formed. It's like taking a photograph that captures a moment in time and never changes. These are the beliefs that cause us problems because they keep us living in the past, not the present. We forever reference the past for who we are today.

But know this: *All beliefs and thoughts can be released or transformed*, even if we took them on at birth or even in the womb. These beliefs are typically about survival. No surprise there. They formed early and deeply, even though we didn't yet have language. We experienced the event and that consciousness became engrained. I believe we add descriptive words later, when we gain language skills. So now, when we go back to the root cause of a belief from birth, the language has become part of that event. The brain has linked that early event, the feelings and emotions we experienced, our consciousness at that moment, and the words about what that meant.

The belief *I'm not good enough* is devastating to one's sense of well-being. When it gets triggered, our whole sense of self can collapse and the decisions we make become based on that poor sense of self. Those decisions may not be very wise because they're actually made from our "child consciousness."

This destructive thinking/feeling underneath impedes our growth, as we become adults, striving to succeed and create a happy life for ourselves. No matter what we create externally for ourselves, this foundational consciousness and experience of being not good enough will show up in our actions.

The Positive Intent of "I'm Not Good Enough" may surprise you, given all the negative impacts just presented. Your belief systems were ALWAYS meant to help you! At the time they were formed, they were always meant to be a positive solution for what was occurring in your life. If they now create problems for you, it's because they are still in their childlike format and haven't been upgraded, or because they were never true to begin with. We hang onto outdated belief systems because they were originally meant to help us, and because we saw them as a solution.

Let's say when you were three years old you got the message from your mother that you were a "bad boy!" You didn't understand that it was your behavior that was upsetting her. You thought it was *You*. Thus, you formed two beliefs: *I'm bad* and *I'm not good enough*.

The common child's thinking goes like this: Being "bad" brings pain and feelings of not being loved. When Mommy is mad at me that means she doesn't love me. However, when I'm good, then I get Mommy to smile and she loves me. So I need to be good to get love. If I know I'm *not* good enough, then I'll *try harder* to be good enough.

The thought *I'm not good enough* is a reminder to be on the lookout for bad behavior and try harder to be good. That's the original positive intent of the belief: to be good and get Mommy's love and approval.

The problem is that *I'm not good enough* is not a pathway to being good enough. Until you release or change this belief, no matter how hard you try to be good, you will still have the belief *I'm not good enough*. Trying harder doesn't erase the underlying belief; it actually reinforces it. As you try harder, and actually do well and are rewarded with approval, the pathway for this belief gets stronger. In your reality, you really are not good enough, so you never let up trying harder to be better. It's a vicious circle, not a virtuous one.

The positive intent of *I'm not good enough* is to be good enough and therefore be accepted and loved, and to avoid the pain of being rejected and not loved. But this mindset doesn't work. All that *I'm not good enough* creates are feelings of shame and worthlessness. It can never, ever, bring feelings of love and approval. It's not a pathway to success even if it does force you to work harder and do better. You may succeed in the outer world, but at a high cost to your inner world, your sense of self-esteem, self-worth, and self-love.

"THERE'S SOMETHING WRONG WITH ME"

A common belief closely linked to *I'm not good enough* is *There's something wrong with me*. This belief also has a profound negative impact on one's sense of worth. I know one woman who created this belief at the moment she was born, when she was held upside down and slapped. Rather than being held and loved, she was put aside into a bassinet away from her mother, who was under anesthesia. There was no bonding, no nursing, no moment of connection. It was a shocking and disruptive event for her. In that moment, she experienced sensations, emotions and energy in the way she was treated. As she grew and developed language, and replayed that original experience in her brain, she added the words *there's something wrong with me*.

During our first years of our life, we see ourselves as the cause of everything that happens outside of us. If someone acts in a certain way, we believe it's about us or because of us. We experience it through our infant perceptions and later we add the language.

This woman's thought ruled her life for 50 years because, when we have such a belief, we attract experiences that reinforce it. Over the years, she searched for what was wrong with her – through therapy, self-help books, and conferences. It was like an itch that she kept scratching. Sometimes, "scratching" make it worse. Sometimes the itch goes away for a while. But it is always there, underneath the façade of "everything's fine." It's a sense of oneself that you can't get rid of.

Here's the thing: Her belief was never true to begin with! There wasn't anything wrong with that baby, or any other newborn. It was her perception of how she was treated. In truth, there was a lot wrong with the way babies born in the 1940-50s were treated. But a newborn doesn't know it was just the procedures the medical establishment was using at that time. There wasn't an emphasis on natural childbirth, or bonding, or nursing, or fathers being present at the birth. It wasn't *ever* about her, and yet, she suffered mental and emotional damage.

She was in yet another workshop about improving her life. This one was about core beliefs that we take on very early in life, often at birth or soon thereafter. The instructor helped the attendees uncover their core belief because we often cannot see the belief ourselves because it's been an integral part of our personality for as long as we can remember. When the instructor suggested *there's something wrong with me* was this woman's core belief, she described it as "a lightning bolt shot through me." She unmistakably saw how that thought had ruled her life. In that sudden *aha* moment, she released that thought's life-long hold on her.

Once she released the belief, poof, it was gone. She then began to see all the ways it had affected her life: always searching for what was really wrong with her, so she could fix it. Now, whenever that thought meanders into her consciousness, she's immediately aware of it and knows it's not true. It holds no power over her. That consciousness no longer controls her sense of Self as it once did.

We are all subject to the effects of these childhood beliefs – until we change them. That's what self-help books are about: how to change our limiting subconscious beliefs and thereby change our life.

There's no rule that says we can't hold opposing beliefs in our subconscious mind. In fact, we have all sorts of variations of beliefs within us. Many of these beliefs relate to certain situations or relationships. For example, you may excel at work, being gifted and capable at what you do. You may manage others and do an excellent job of directing and leading your group to success. You don't have any thought of not being good enough at work.

But, at home – where you're a mother or father, husband or wife – you may show up as a very different person. You may appear to not do anything right. Your spouse may point out ways you are lacking. Or you may demonstrate poor parenting skills – losing your temper, yelling at the kids, unable to keep the household in order. At work, you think clearly and focus on the end result. At home, your mind gets cluttered and your plans for a happy family life disintegrate.

You wonder, what's wrong with me? How can I be two such different people – one so effective and one so overwhelmed? The reason is that you have subconscious beliefs specific to each role and relationship – and these beliefs can be diametrically opposed to each other.

If you find yourself being "two different people," look at your beliefs in each situation. These beliefs are not difficult to find. They actually play out right in front of you, depending on the role you are playing. You may have trouble seeing the beliefs yourself, because they look and feel like the truth. If so, try pretending you are a neutral third party and stand back and look at your life.

The Positive Intent of "Something's Wrong With Me" was very similar to the previous *I'm not enough.* It was meant to help you find out what was wrong, fix it, and then be loved and accepted, or safe from being punished.

If you remember nothing else from this book, remember this: *You, the Soul of who you are, are Love. At your core, you are perfect.* We are all eternal souls who are temporarily here in human form. From the human viewpoint, we all have habits, behaviors and thoughts that are less than desirable, unacceptable, and some would even call evil. That's the human side of us.

When we die, we release the human form and return to our Higher Self, which is Love. Then we remember, "Ah yes, I am Love." Then you can remember, "There never was anything wrong with me. I just thought there was." It's better, however, for you to remember now, in your human form, so that you can learn what you came here to learn: It's all about Love.

"I GET ABANDONED"

Abandonment – another common limiting belief – is the thought or feeling of being left, discarded, not cared for, or not supported emotionally, physically, or mentally. It's that sense of being alone in the world and needing to make it on your own because no one else is there for you.

Abandonment beliefs usually start in childhood, often very early, when you feel as though one or both of your parents simply are not there for you. Perhaps a parent leaves through a divorce or death, is simply away at work, or goes into a hospital for a short stay. All types of situations can cause children to perceive that someone they expected to be there for them in a caring and supportive way has abandoned them.

This belief can also form in everyday situations. I once worked with a man in his forties who had the ongoing pattern of women in his life leaving him. He saw himself as an abandoned lover. In going back to the root cause, he saw himself as a young boy about 3 or 4 years old in the grocery store with his mother. This was back in the 1950s when there were no fears of children being harmed or kidnapped. As his mother shopped, she walked around to the adjoining aisle, while he focused on something in his aisle. All of a sudden, he looked up and thought, "Where's my mother?" He immediately went into fear, panic, and shock. "She's gone!" In that moment, he took on the belief, "*Women leave me.*" It didn't matter that she was just in the next aisle. That moment of panic got etched into his subconscious, and then began to replay throughout his life.

With this strong, energized belief in his subconscious, he unconsciously attracted women who had a belief that fit his belief – like a hand and a glove. The women he brought into his life believed, *I need to leave before I get hurt.* What a match! They lived out their belief by leaving him, and he lived out his belief by feeling abandoned.

This scenario may seem too crazy to be true, but it is very, very true. Just think about it. Does it bring up any thoughts in your mind about any relationships you have had?

This is how simply beliefs can get formed and take on permanence. Over and over I've seen a limiting belief formed in one moment – and the situation is completely resolved a minute or two later – but that's too late. The belief has already been ener-gized. For some reason, the little boy's limiting belief was not replaced by the truth that Mom was right there, and he was getting hugged within a minute. In many cases, the truth does not override or correct the misperception or reduce the intensity of the fear. That's when the limiting belief becomes a magnet for life, manifesting itself over and over.

Feeling abandoned causes a lot of heartache. So does believ-ing you need to leave before you get hurt. My clients are often surprised, amazed, and then even angry to find out that the root cause of so much of their pain and suffering has been caused by something so simple. To add salt to their wound, they find that their intense belief wasn't even true to begin with. They expected the root cause of their emotional pain to be something worthy, or traumatic, or horrible. They wanted to justify their belief of being abandoned or needing to leave. I have discovered that many people find it very difficult to accept that the root cause was just a moment in time. Even worse, it was just a child's misperception.

A common cause of feeling abandoned comes from being an infant in the crib, alone in the dark, crying for someone to come. When mother doesn't come to pick you up *in that moment*, you, the baby, feel alone, uncared for, and abandoned. If all these feel-ing get locked into your subconscious mind, and are not changed, your abandonment story begins.

If you're a parent and you're worried about the limiting beliefs your child may be forming, please know this: You *cannot* protect your children from forming limiting beliefs because you cannot begin to imagine what's going on in their head. What you can do is change your own limiting beliefs, so as not to pass these beliefs on to them. Furthermore, since we are all connected, by changing your own limiting beliefs, you help others change theirs.

If you suffer from this idea that you've been abandoned, and you really believe it's true, I'd like you to step back and realize something else: The *only thing* that is actually true is that you have a *belief* that you were abandoned. Your belief, thought, perception, feeling, and experiences of abandonment make this statement appear true to you. But that's not the truth.

In fact, even the cause of your belief was not necessarily true. That mother did not abandon her son in the store. She simply went into the next aisle. The other mother did not abandon the child in the crib. She came a few moments later and picked up her child.

Even if the three-year-old boy had truly been abandoned in the store, generalizing that experience to his being abandoned by women for the rest of his life was never an appropriate follow-on thought. His experience was a moment in time at age three. That's all. It was not the blueprint for how all women would treat him.

Consider the little girl crying to be picked up. Her mother was in the other room, and came to soothe her upset baby as soon as she could – just moments later. But that part of the story gets forgotten or ignored. Think about it. Of course your mother, or some other person, would pick you up when you were crying.

I had a client who, at age two, formed a similar belief during an adult party. Everyone was so high above this child, who was way down on the floor. She felt not seen and abandoned. So she cried and formed the beliefs, *I'm abandoned, no one cares about me.* It took some time in a session for her to realize the obvious: Of course she had been picked up. There was no way on earth that a crying child in the midst of adults was not going to be picked up.

It's common sense. But when the belief is strong, common sense and the adult perspective are nowhere to be found. The believer doesn't even think to question the belief.

I'd like you to really take note of this: *Never ever are the thoughts or perceptions of a three-year-old valid for a person in their thirties, forties, fifties, or older!* They are appropriate for the child, and may be true at that age. But they are not appropriate or true for the adult because they are not adult thoughts. What you thought in childhood should not be running your life today.

So even if a parent had actually left the home and was gone from the child's daily life, that didn't mean that parent abandoned the child. It sure looked that way, didn't it? But what was actually true was that the parent left, or died, or moved. Or even more likely, the parent left for work for the day! This could be traumatic for a young child, even when siblings or a babysitter were still in the home. If he believed *I've been abandoned*, he might even expand that belief to not trusting his parents to be there for him, or to fulfill his needs, because he'd begged them to stay, yet still they left for work.

People can also feel abandoned by God/the Universe. This, too, can begin even at the moment of birth when the shock of being born into a little physical body causes an infant to feel separate from the Oneness and Love it just left on a Soul level.

Imagine that's you. You, the Soul, know Oneness with Source and All That Is. It's the natural state of Being for all of us. Yet when you get into the body, the experience of being physically separated morphs into being spiritually separated, and thus alone. This is an existential feeling that most people have: the feeling of being Alone, separate from Source. For some, this then shifts into feeling abandoned by Source, left here on earth to make it on one's own.

In Reality, we are never separate from Source, although we may feel separated. To say you are separate from Source is like saying you are separate from air. You can't be separate from air. It moves in and through you, giving you life. Similarly, you can't be separate from the Essence of God/Source, because this essence is in every cell of your body. You are an expression of Source and therefore never separate, regardless of what it feels like to be in a human body. It's part of our journey to come to this realization that Source breathes us and we are One with All That Is. That is equally true for every person on planet Earth.

The Positive Intent of "I've Been Abandoned." So what might have been the positive intent of taking on beliefs such as *I'm all alone, There's no one here for me, I'm not supported,* or *I've been abandoned*? This is a common set of beliefs that leads to feeling isolated and abandoned, even when you're in a loving family or have strong friendships. You sense that you are alone in the world and you must make it on your own because no one else is there for you. What a tragic situation: You can have love all around you, yet you feel isolated.

Referring back to the story of the man in his forties who had the ongoing pattern of women in his life leaving him, he was always being abandoned in his love relationships. He was the child in the grocery story whose mother was in the next aisle when he suddenly thought, *"She's gone."*

His experience of fear and panic was so intense that he immediately created a defense mechanism. While it all happened in the blink of an eye, when he was later under hypnosis, he was able to replay the experience and recognize his thinking at that time. It went along these lines: "I never want to experience this shock and surprise again. It's too terrible. But this is how life is: Mom Left Me! If I know that's what happens in life, then I won't be surprised next time, and I'll be able to handle it better. I never want to feel this same terrible feeling again."

The positive intent of his thinking was to never again feel the terrible shock and panic of realizing Mom has left him. So he guards himself against that happening by preparing for it by believing *women leave me*. The problem with his rationale, however, is that this belief has had the opposite effect of what he wants.

This often happens with our limiting beliefs: They end up becoming the cause of the problem we were trying to solve. Through time and misinterpretation, they become contaminated. This man has vibrated his energized belief that women leave him out into the world, which has drawn that circumstance into his life again and again. What he really has wanted is to protect himself against women leaving him. But the opposite has happened because each time a woman has left him, it has reinforced his belief, making it seem even truer, and also sending an even louder signal out to the universe.

When he released his habitual way of thinking about being left by women, he then found he needed to do inner work around his own behaviors in relationships, so that he wouldn't set up situations to encourage the woman to leave. He was then able to move into healthier, longer-term relationships.

"WHY DID HE (OR SHE) REJECT ME?"

Rejection is similar to abandonment – and often connected to it. Rejection can feel more personal than abandonment because a person or persons have rejected you personally, cast you aside. Once, they were there for you. Now, they've rejected you. If they tell you exactly why they don't want to be with you, they make their actions all about you, which can be painful, stabbing, traumatic, and dramatic.

If you feel rejected, go back and read the entire abandonment section; replace "abandonment" with your story of rejection. It will all fit because rejection is still based on your underlying beliefs about who you are and how others treat you. It's a story you tell yourself. You may even expect it to happen because it always has. You live out this reality.

How do you respond to direct attacks on your character? Do these character assassinations get inside your mind, cause chaos, and disrupt your thinking, your emotions, your self-concept, your self-worth, and your view of the world? Even though you know these debilitating thoughts about your character are not true, do you still accept them and live by them? That's very common, and you would likely reply, "Of course! That person I cared about is attacking me! How can I not take it personally?"

Yes, of course it can hurt, and you can feel it moving through your mind and body. You can experience different intensities of hurt: as a sting, as a stab to your heart, even as being tortured. The sensations can last for a short time, minutes or hours, days or weeks, or even years.

I worked with one client who remains angry, bitter, resentful, and revengeful twenty years after feeling rejected in a divorce. Can you imagine twenty years of toxic emotions running through your mind and body? It's more common than you think. Look at your own life. See if you can bring up hurts from childhood and feel strong emotions connected to a memory.

The Positive Intent of "Why Did He (or She) Reject Me?" What on earth could have been the positive intent of this belief? You're going to find it's a very similar theme for many of these beliefs: self-protection. To the child, it comes down to this: "It's the unexpectedness of being rejected that causes me so much pain. If I know what to expect from life, I won't be surprised and it won't hurt so much. Since I know that I am going to be rejected, I can numb myself against future losses and hurts. I can reduce my pain by simply watching and waiting for it to happen. That's how I will protect myself."

Of course, thinking this belief will protect you is not the truth. But it is the truth from the child's perspective, and it is that perception which continues on into adulthood.

What I have learned is this: Anything anyone says to you – especially in anger or in any strong emotion – is actually about them. It will also be about you in some way, but it is certainly about them. You have just hit one of their hot buttons and they explode. They spew out onto you the perceptions, beliefs, emotions they dislike in themselves. This is called projection.

The other side of the coin is just as true. Anytime you spew anger and venom onto someone else – saying it's all about them and what they've done and who they are – take a deep breath and realize it's really all your stuff, your projections, and your beliefs.

We are each a mirror for one another. When you say anything about another, it's as though you're looking into a mirror and saying all those things about yourself. This may not be obvious to you at first, but take a good look inside and you'll find it's true in some form or another. Rejection from another is about them. You rejecting another is all about you.

We all have options on how to respond to being rejected. In the moment, you can breathe through the experience, and notice how you're responding. Pay attention to what is being said to you and about you. Then take a look at this criticism. Does it have any merit, truth, or partial truth? You can use the situation as a positive learning experience, rather than take it personally and get stuck on it for years.

There's truth in the old saying that when you point a finger at someone, you have three fingers pointing back at you. When you blame someone else, look to see how you are the same – and how much you really dislike that characteristic in yourself.

For instance, if you are calling someone rude, ignorant, and self-centered, in that moment, look to see if you are being rude (passing judgment), ignorant (not knowing all the facts as the other person sees them), and self-centered (looking from only your own point of view).

One of the best books to help you see this clearly is by don Miguel Ruiz, *The Four Agreements*. It's been around since 1997 and is a classic on helping people understand not to take anything personally, as we all think and act from our own wounds and beliefs.

I recently watched a segment of a talk show in which one of the hosts talked about being on a conference call. She called in early and was surprised to hear the other three people were already on the call. They were not aware that she had joined in the call and they continued talking – about her. She listened in as they honestly – and rather brutally – talked about her looks, her abilities, and her talent. She took notes on everything they were saying. "How often do you get a chance to really hear what others feel about you?" Rather than reject them or feel victimized by what she heard, she used their remarks as feedback. She made the decision to not work with these people, but rather to pursue her own path. That decision led her to eventually become a host on a popular talk show – her real calling in life.

So if someone is rejecting or blaming you, don't discount every-thing that person is saying. Look to see where there's some truth. Taking on all their energy and venom is not your only choice. You can choose to *not* take it on; rather see it in it's true light. That person is hurting inside and they are projecting their pain onto you. Perhaps you hurt them. If so, look at your own behaviors. You can learn how you affect others by listening to their reactions. Regardless of who did what to whom, you have a choice of ways to listen and respond. Use it to your benefit.

"I'M AFRAID"

Fear will always show up when we are moving into new terri-tory in our life. It's a natural part of our growth. Fear lets us know that we are at the edge of our comfort zone. It will show up as we continue to push our boundaries into new areas of experimenta-tion, success, and achievement.

So, while fear is natural, there's one very big problem....

Most of our fears are not adult-based fears, nor are they based on what is actually happening in our life now. They are our child-hood fears being replayed and replayed. Everyone has fears formed in childhood. You could be three years old and hear your parents fighting in the middle of the night. You get terrified and hide under your covers, staying very still, closing out the sounds of their loud voices. That entire moment can be programmed into your subconscious mind and become your blueprint for how to stay safe. It was your truth in that moment: *I'm safe hiding under these covers staying absolutely still and quiet.* The terror feels so big within you, and you know there's nothing you can do to make them stop fighting, or to bring peace into the household. The fear can feel bigger than you, overwhelming you, and you feel powerless.

What terrifies you, this child, is the thought that the parents will stop liking each other and one or both of them will leave – and then what will happen to you? Who will take care of you? Ultimately, these thoughts lead to *I'm going to die!* That feels very real to a child. *I'm going to die because there's no one to take care of me.*

Such highly charged emotions and thoughts are readily programmed into the mind – where they may stay for years, or decades. Anytime fear feels bigger than you, or overwhelming, or if it's gone beyond fear into terror, know that you are replaying a childhood fear. It's not a current fear. It's an old habitual fear. It's not the truth. Just because your fear *feels* real doesn't mean it *is* the truth. Plain and simple, it is not the truth.

All of this experience can replay throughout your life, making you terrified of moving out from under the covers and into new experiences. You will fall back into this old habitual fear over and over again. And each time, the fear can feel stronger and bigger within you, keeping you frozen from moving into new experiences in your life. You can't breathe, you can't think straight, and your whole world seems to be falling apart. It has become very real and very physical. This is not just in your mind. At this point, you doubt and question yourself. Underneath it all is the subconscious (or perhaps conscious) thinking, *"If I do this (move, change jobs, begin a new relationship, start a business), I won't survive, I'll fail, I won't have enough money, I'm powerless to make it happen… I'll die."*

Fear keeps us stuck from moving ahead by taking us out into a future and "making up what might happen." We totally make up all the things that can go wrong, even though they may be legitimate possibilities. Then we believe what we just made up as though it were actually going to happen! We give meaning to our world through the stories we make up in our minds.

Let me say this again because it's what we typically do: We make up a story about what might happen (bad things) and then we believe that story (we make it feel real and true) and take actions based on what we made up (don't do anything, stay stuck). We make our story "real", and then act upon it.

There are endless possibilities that could occur in the future. Our real future depends largely on our actions, our consciousness, and our intentions – as well as factors that are completely out of our control and, as yet, completely unknown.

If you're going to make up fearful stories about what bad might happen – call it the "Big What If" – then at least do yourself the courtesy of making up a positive "Big What If," and feel it just as intensely. *Both* scenarios are possibilities. Acknowledge that! You can begin to de-energize your fearful stories by countering them just as quickly and powerfully with positive stories. As you move out of the belief systems that create your fear, you'll find that using your mind to create positive scenarios is far more helpful, creative, and life enhancing.

I'm in a coaching program with a wonderful and very capable woman, Felicia Searcy, www.feliciasearcy.com, who has been mentored by Mary Morrissey, also an amazing woman who has walked through the fires of life and now is teaching people how to live their dreams.

During a coaching call with Felicia, I had an *aha* moment about "what if." In our homework, we had written down our five biggest fears. During the call, I looked at my homework and realized that four of my five fears started with "what if ..." and then some terrible outcome. I had never consciously realized how that "what if" was such a big part of my fear thinking.

Felicia gave me a few alternatives to "stare down" my what-if fears: One, as described above, list your 5 top fears. Two, do some positive what-if scenarios – and feel them vividly. Three, an even more powerful tactic, which Felicia learned in her own life: in the face of your greatest fear, tell yourself, "If that happens, my God and I will handle it."

Isn't that an absolutely amazing response to your greatest fear? And isn't it the truth! Somehow, you have already walked through fires of life. Somehow, you have handled everything in your life because you are still alive. True, some of life hasn't been graceful or positive, but somehow you have handled it and learned to grow stronger and more resilient.

"My God and I will handle it." Those words can diminish any fear and any story you may tell yourself, if you will just believe the words and live them when you most need them.

The Positive Intent of "I'm Afraid" was to keep you safe. If you were afraid, you wouldn't do anything and then you wouldn't get hurt. It's usually that simple. But, today, if it's still there, in your subconscious, it's not keeping you safe. It's keeping you from moving forward.

"I HAVE TO...I SHOULD...I CAN'T...I DON'T WANT TO"

How deadening it is to have your days run by the constant nagging thoughts of *I have to, I should, I can't,* or *I don't want to.* These beliefs control the lives of far too many people. Are you one of those who lives by your "to do" list, which always includes much more than you could possibly do in a day? At the end of the day, do you think, *"Ohhh, I didn't finish everything I needed to"*? As you're starting one errand, do you suddenly decide you should squeeze in three more? Are you always behind in what you want to accomplish? Even when you do finish a project, are you only thinking about the next five things on your list? Or, are you the opposite? Do you procrastinate, putting off doing what you need to do, ending up accomplishing next to nothing at the end of the day?

If these questions resonate with you, then your life is controlled by such beliefs as:

- "I'm always having to play catch up."

- "I absolutely must do one more thing."

- "There are so many demands on my time that I feel overwhelmed."

- "I never seem to be doing what I need/want to do."

- "Time is never on my side. There's never enough time."

You might think this way of living isn't really based on a belief system because it's your actual life experience. Yes, this can be your daily experience. However, you live this way because in your subconscious are beliefs that you have to, you should, etc.

I've had numerous clients with these beliefs whose typical root cause was based in having to do chores as a child. Using hypnosis to go back to this root cause, these clients had the same experience: *I have to do this... and it's boring or hard... and it takes forever ...., and I want to go out and play, but I can't.* This pattern became entrenched in their subconscious mind as *"this is how life is."* Every day or week the house had to be cleaned, the lawn mowed, meals cooked, homework done, pets fed, younger siblings watched, and so on. This mindset has been repeated ever since.

As adults, these clients have "chores" (errands, work projects, children's needs, social obligations, etc.), that take forever (every day there's more to do, never ending), and they can't have fun until it's all done (no time to enjoy their days or evenings because of the guilt and stress of all that *needs* to be done first).

Can you see that it's the same pattern as in childhood? I call it the "cookie cutter" effect. The pattern in childhood creates a cookie cutter, and then each cookie is cut from that mold and looks exactly the same. You recreate the same pattern throughout your life. And yes, you have many things to do in your life and it's all necessary, and so on.

Here's the thing to remember: Your life is the way it is now because you are repeating the patterns from childhood with your thinking.

I have a good friend who was always running around frantically in the morning trying to get to work on time. Invariably, she was stressed and not feeling particularly good about herself by the time she arrived at work. So I suggested she begin to "play" with time, to find out for herself how her perceptions and use of time were an illusion and based on her beliefs. So she began to tell herself the affirmation, "I have all the time I need in the morning, including time for a cup of tea."

She did this for several weeks and then reported back to me, "I don't know quite how this works, but now I have time for myself in the mornings. I didn't consciously change my routine, except that now I sit down and enjoy a cup of tea before going off to work."

External situations are not causing you stress. The real stresses come from your out-of-date thinking about life. You feel disempowered (like a child who has no choice but to do the chores), or overwhelmed (it's too much for a child to do or it's actually work the parent should do), or thinking you have to be perfect (you, the child, get in trouble if the house isn't cleaned to mother's demanding standards).

If you procrastinate, think back to when you were a child. Did you get things done or try to put them off? Many times procrastination is also linked to not wanting to do chores or homework, so you went and did something else much more fun.

The Positive Intent of "I Have To… I Should… I Can't… I Don't Want To" was to get you to behave in a way that would gain you love, approval, safety, or security. By knowing you had to, or should, do something, then you would do it, perhaps saving yourself from being punished.

On the other hand, "I can't" and "I don't want to" enabled the child to have a voice in his or her life. Rather than being ruled by an adult world, the child began to say what he or she would or would not do. Autonomy, which is having a say in one's life or being self-governing, is a basic need that everyone has. As part of child development, this desire to say "NO!" gets very strong in two year olds. Have you noticed that?

"I'M STUCK"

I often have clients come to me and simply state their issue as: *I'm stuck. I can't move forward in my life.* This can be rooted in childhood beliefs of: *I'm not smart enough* or *I'm not as smart as the others* or *I can't do anything right.*

One client had older brothers who would tell him what to do, so he would wait for them to give him instructions. He was three years old and in charge of guarding the candy he and his older brothers had put in their fort. He got bored and left the fort. When some neighborhood kids came and stole the candy, his brothers blamed him and beat him up. From that childhood event, he formed the beliefs, *I can't do anything right. I need to have them tell me what to do.*

As an adult, he was still waiting for others to tell him what to do in his career. He hadn't moved up in his field, although he was quite capable and had years of experience. He was afraid to be the boss because his childhood habit of following his brothers to school and to sports became programmed into his subconscious as: *This is how life is: I follow others and do what they tell me to do.*

At the time I worked with him, he had been unemployed for over a year, feeling stuck.

In going back to the root cause of being stuck, he went back to a memory at four years of age when he followed his older brothers out to play, but they went on ahead of him. He stood at a fence, afraid to cross the street and afraid to go back home. Staying at the fence felt safe. That pattern of being afraid to move forward because it didn't feel safe was still active in him decades later.

After releasing several similar limiting beliefs during a session, along with the energy and emotions attached to them, he moved ahead in his life and got a job in his chosen field of work. His beliefs that had controlled his thinking and behaviors for over 40 years dissolved in just one hour.

As another example, when a child does poorly in school, or doesn't get a perfect grade or report card, the results can be devastating. The child can feel it deeply, scared they've disappointed their parents or their teacher, or afraid the other kids in school will find out. This fear can translate into adult fear of failure. They believe they're not going to succeed because they don't know enough, so they settle for jobs that are not fulfilling. They're afraid to step up to a new job because they "won't know what they're doing" in that new job. This fear is the child's elementary school experience replaying in their mind, telling them to hold back because it's not worth the pain of being rejected or failing in that new job.

The fear *I don't know enough* even rises up strongly in them when they just *think* about stepping out of the job they dislike and moving into another job or starting their own business. Their desire to move on is strong, but their fear is stronger. It's enough to keep them stuck for years on end.

The Positive Intent of "I'm Stuck" was often safety and/or acceptance. In families where there was chaos or a lot of disruption, a child often learned to be very still, shrink back, hide, or just be quiet to become invisible in order to feel safe.

Children with these beliefs often hold themselves back, thinking: *Don't speak up,* or *Don't be in charge,* or *Don't move ahead because I may be wrong.* They often think that other kids won't like them if they're smarter or achieve more, so they don't do any homework or don't turn it in on time. Their desire to be part of their peer group overshadows their inner drive to succeed.

"I'M ALONE...I'M ALL ON MY OWN...I DON'T BELONG"

It rather amazes me how many clients form the belief *I'm on my own, there's no one here for me* in early childhood, sometimes by the time they're three or four. They can feel all grown up at this early age, as though they're capable of taking care of themselves – which, of course, is not true. Children who form this belief can actually think they are alone, absolutely believing there's no parent or adult anywhere around to take care of them.

This belief can form from one moment in time when the parent is in another room, or the child wakes up in the middle of the night and feels alone. That deep feeling of being alone gets recorded, along with the consequence of *so that means I'm on my own* – even though nothing could be further from the truth. Obviously, young children are never in charge of their own care, no matter what they believe. But this feeling of being alone and having to do everything all on their own can become a theme in their life.

As adults, they can be happily married to a supportive spouse, and yet still feel alone and having to do "it" (that is, "life") all by themselves. Or, they can go the other direction and actually remain alone or single, perhaps as a single parent. They are playing out the belief *It's all up to me,* raising their children, providing housing, and making decisions on their own. Even when surrounded by friends and loved ones, they can feel alone, isolated, repeating that momentary feeling they had as a young child.

Clients who feel as though they don't belong – a kindred limiting belief – often go back to elementary school days as the root cause of that belief. They didn't fit in at school, they wore different clothes than the other kids, they moved and so were "the new kid" part way through the school year, or they were younger than siblings, and so felt left out. However it began, that feeling has stayed with them into adulthood.

When one client changed that belief, he reported back that he could feel a difference. He was at a social gathering, and even though he was standing back and watching, he didn't feel isolated or alone as he had in the past. His behavior of staying "outside the action" remained pretty much the same, but inside himself, he now felt part of the group, which was quite different for him. He said the old feeling of being alone simply wasn't there any more.

The Positive Intent of "I'm Alone" was also about survival. Children who took on the limiting belief *I'm all alone* did so for a good reason (at the time): They did it when they believed that surviving was all up to them. In their perception, a safe adult was not available to them, so they took on that role by themselves, or so they thought. This was ALL in the child's mind. There was an adult present, even if they were not being a reliable parent. Four-year-olds CANNOT take care of themselves even if that's their thinking. But by taking on this type of belief, they felt safe inside and believed they would survive on their own.

"I CAN'T SPEAK UP"

Learning to speak up in the face of fear can be terrifying. I have had numerous clients who are very afraid to speak up in a group. They tend to be fine one-on-one or with a few others, but not in larger groups. In the case of one woman, whenever she or her siblings spoke up as children, they got slapped hard in the face and were told to shut up. This is how subconscious beliefs get so deeply rooted. For her, staying quiet and out of trouble was imperative. It wasn't safe to speak up. That fear has remained with her. As an adult, she was still afraid and anxious to speak up, especially in a professional setting. When a fear is this strong and prevalent, you can be sure it's part of what you have come in to experience and learn in this lifetime.

With another client, he was afraid to speak up because life was very confusing for him and he was afraid he would add to his mother's sadness concerning another sibling. He remembered one time when he said what was on his mind, his mother became quite distressed and he didn't understand why. So he made the decision to remain silent in order not to upset her ever again.

I also find this fear of speaking up prevalent in people from alcoholic families. If one of the parents was drunk, the children didn't want to do or say anything to set that parent off onto a tirade. The fear kept these children paralyzed, silent, still. They didn't want to get hit or in trouble by saying or doing the slightest "wrong" thing. They quickly learned that peace in the household depended on their being quiet. Their learned response translates into the adult behaviors of not being able to speak up for oneself, especially with authority figures (such as at work), or around men (or women), depending on which parent was the alcoholic. They still fear they will get in trouble if they speak up.

The Positive Intent of "I Can't Speak Up" was similar to the limiting beliefs of *I'm stuck* and *I'm alone*. Some children took on *I can't speak up* to protect themselves or others from harm. It was a survival belief, and the child might have had a very good reason for adhering to it. You may continue to create situations in which

83

you don't feel safe speaking up, so the belief can continue to look and feel valid to you. Here's what's true though: You are not five years old any longer, and you can speak from your authentic voice, which others will listen to and respect.

"I DON'T MATTER....I'M NOT WORTHY"

I've noticed that quite often, along with the above belief of I don't belong, the belief I don't matter forms when a baby is born and the former youngest child – age two, three or four years old – feels displaced. This older sibling is no longer the main attraction, the one getting the special attention, the one held on mother's lap, or the one whom the grandparents go to first. Suddenly, there's someone "more special" in the home, which the older child translates into feeling less than, not needed, superfluous.

One woman was three when her younger sibling was born. Her thoughts were, "What's wrong with me that they needed another child? I don't matter anymore." This feeling of being less than, not worthy of attention, became an under-current that was always present for her, in spite of how well she did in life or how happy she might feel at times. She always felt this "truth" underneath, and would hold herself back from achieving the success she was capable of attaining.

The real truth of our journey in life is that we are all already fully worthy because we are part of Source Essence: We are an expression of God. In Christianity it's stated, "We are the sons and daughters of the Living God." We can't be any more worthy because that's our inherent nature.

The problem is that we can feel less worthy. All of our limiting beliefs simply make us feel less: less worthy, less loved, less accepted. Our journey is to realize that these "less than" beliefs are not true. In truth, we are spiritual beings in physical bodies, fully worthy.

The Positive Intent of "I Don't Matter" was the opposite of what actually occurred. As a child, if we told ourselves, *I don't matter,* then we thought it wouldn't hurt so badly when we felt ignored or less important than our younger sibling.

By now I'm sure you're seeing a theme with all of these positive intents. The child's mind takes on these beliefs to circumvent pain, loss, or feeling not safe. The limiting belief is meant to somehow protect against feeling unloved or unsafe. The thinking goes further: If we are unloved, then perhaps we'll be thrown out of the family or no one will take care of us…and we'll die. It is this unspoken and underlying threat of dying that keeps so many of these limiting beliefs intact into adulthood, hidden from our conscious mind.

"I CAN'T DO IT RIGHT"

This also shows up in one's life as *I never get what I want* or *it never works out for me.* I've had clients brought to deep and sudden sadness when this belief is triggered. They're attempting to access some information in a session and then "wham!" they start crying, "See, I can't do anything right. It never works out for me!" They are instantly in despair and hopelessness.

They've accessed a belief they acquired quite young, often in the toddler or preschool years. This belief can begin when a young child is intent on coloring in a coloring book but can't seem to stay inside the lines of the drawing. An adult may correct the child, explaining that in order to color correctly, they need to keep their crayon marks inside the lines of the pre-drawn objects. It's such a small incident, but that's enough for the child to despair inside, deciding, *I can't do it right*. That can be the beginning of a lifelong pattern of frustration as they live out the experiences of this belief.

I had one client who, when she was a child, was told she could have one special toy of her choice while on vacation. She chose a toy that she liked. However, the next day, in a store window, she saw the doll of her dreams. But it was too late. She'd already chosen her one toy. She didn't get to have her dream doll.

This experience made such a deep impression on her that she could easily remember the incident vividly when I worked with her. She formed two companion beliefs, *I can't do it right* (choosing the wrong toy) and *I don't get what I want* (dream doll), and the combination of these two beliefs created *it never works out for me*.

She relived these beliefs over and over throughout her life, each time adding more credence to their "truth" in her life. The sad part is: none of them was true to begin with. Just because she found a toy more to her liking the next day didn't mean she hadn't chosen her first toy well. Based on what she knew of the toys available that day, she had made a good decision. But her desire for her dream doll made the "I can't do it right" experience "stick" in her programming and take over as "the law" of how her life would be from that day forward.

The Positive Intent of "I Can't Do It Right" was (1) to remind the child to try harder to get it right the first time, and then (2) to help alleviate the feelings of despair and low self-worth when they made a mistake. But this positive intent won't lead to the desired positive outcome because these two intents work against each other. The first intent: *If I know I'm not going to do it right, then*

I'll work harder might lead the child to do something right the first time, yes. However, lurking behind this positive intent is the second intent: *If I do mess up, it won't hurt as badly because I'll be expecting it,* which sabotages the first positive intent by trying to cushion the blow of not being right the first time There won't be the sudden surprise and disappointment that comes from expecting things to *not* work out. The child's thinking is: expecting the undesired outcome helps lessen the pain. None of this is true, of course. But it's still quite common thinking from the child's point of view.

"I NEED TO BE IN CONTROL"

You may have grown up in a critical household and made the decision to never be like that because it was so hurtful. As the child, you likely formed beliefs that people are critical, or that being critical is a natural response in life. Your conscious decision to not criticize others may not release your original critical belief; so instead, you turn your beliefs against yourself. You become highly self-critical, perfectionist, believing you never do things well enough, over-achieving so you won't make any mistakes, and so on.

On a subconscious level, you likely combine several beliefs – such as being critical, not good enough, and not smart enough – thus making these combined beliefs even more powerful and even more limiting.

These intertwined limiting beliefs become a dominant paradigm for how you show up in the world. And all the while, you pride yourself on not criticizing others verbally. Isn't that ironic how we can think one thing yet do the opposite?

If you believe you do not *verbally* criticize others, look to see how much you *mentally* criticize them. The extent to which you react to others who are critical likely matches the extent to which you are critical within – of yourself and others. Even when you're not the same as your parents, some of the conditions from your childhood unconsciously remain part of you *until* you become conscious of them and then change them.

If you grew up in a household in which your mother was very controlling, you could have taken on any of the following beliefs (and relationships):

- *Being controlling is how I can get what I want.* With this belief, you can end up being like your mother in your own familial relationships.

- *I never want to be controlling, to not have that sort of power play in my relationships.* You may therefore become a people pleaser or a doormat – that is, you don't speak up for what you really want.

- *I'm going to control myself.* With this belief, you may become the perfectionist in the family, making sure your spouse and children are always doing exactly the right thing and looking exactly the right way.

The Positive Intent of "I Need to Be in Control" was to make sense of the chaos around you or the feeling of helplessness. As a child, if you could bring control into your life, as least according to the way you thought about life, then it wouldn't be so chaotic or unsafe. The need to have everything *perfect*, absolutely perfect, brought a feeling of safety and security because you would know what to expect. None of the unexpected surprises or behaviors of others in your family could catch you off guard or harm you.

Being in control, having a sense of extreme order, meant that you could feel safe.

"I'VE BEEN ABUSED"

If you experienced or witnessed abuse in childhood, your resulting beliefs will eventually show up in your relationships. If you were sexually abused as a child, for example, and haven't done enough healing work to release the beliefs and negative energy caused by that abuse, then you will recreate being abused in some way or you may actually become the abuser in adult relationships.

Interestingly, such abuse doesn't always show up as aggressive. It can be subtle abuse, such as the misuse of sex and intimacy. For example, your relationships may lack intimacy on any real or sustained level – which can show up in opposing ways. You may, for instance, become involved with someone who doesn't want to have sex. Or, opposite that, you may find yourself involved with a sex addict. Either way, you lack intimacy and deep connection.

On the other hand, you may be the one who doesn't want to have sex, even though your partner desires it. You may think you want it, yet you find yourself withdrawing from sexual relationships for longer and longer periods of time. Or you may be a sex addict and desire many partners, and yet can't really be intimate in any of them, especially in your primary relationship. The sex is unfulfilling, the emotional emptiness inside doesn't get filled up, and still you are driven to have more partners. Your limiting belief around sex can also take the form of pornography, spending hours and hours on Internet porn sites, watching porn DVDs, buying adult magazines, or frequenting stripper bars.

Sexual abuse in childhood, whether it was just once or countless times over a period of years, and whether it was by someone you knew or a complete stranger, will have lifelong consequences – unless and until you acknowledge it and work on it therapeutically to release or balance the emotions and beliefs it caused that are still trapped in your belief system.

The myriad of beliefs taken on as a result of childhood abuse is insidious because they strike at your very core: your self-concept and safety in the world.

- If the abuse came from a family member or friend, you may have formed beliefs around betrayal and not being able to trust those you should be able to trust. You can form the belief, *Those who love me, hurt me.* You may believe that, fundamentally, the world is not a safe place for you.

- If an adult abused you when you were three or four years old, you didn't have physical power, mental power, or emotional power. You were just a small child caught in a situation with very few resources. You may have taken on the belief *I am powerless,* which is a common theme among those who have been abused because it was true at the time of the abuse.

- If you were threatened with silence, then you had a double dose of not feeling safe: It was not safe to speak up, and in not speaking up, the abuse was allowed to continue.

The Positive Intent of "I've Been Abused" could have been protection, to resolve to "never let this happen to me again." The belief was meant to lead a person out of feeling and acting like a victim and into being self-reliant and no longer abused. But this belief could also have been meant as a cry for help from the child, to let a safe adult know that something has happened that requires adult aid. Remember, this is all from the young child's perspective. There wasn't a lot of consciousness going on in the mind of the child, just the knowledge "this is what happened." As a result, the belief is a reflection of the child's external circumstances, with the mind taking on the thinking of *this is how life is for me; I've been abused.*

This belief can be difficult to even imagine connecting to a positive intent because it's such absolutely unacceptable behavior. But it is the child's thoughts about the behavior that are meant to somehow help the child. By knowing that they are abused, the child can make plans to avoid the abuser, if possible, or as with so many of the beliefs described, prepare himself or herself for living life that includes more abuse.

"LIFE ISN'T FAIR"

I've found that many times clients form the belief that *Life isn't fair* because they had older siblings who got to stay up later than they did. As children, this is how life can look to us: Life isn't fair. This belief can become a central theme in our life, even though we do a tremendous amount of self-healing.

We may not even see this belief in ourselves because it's such a foundational belief. To us, it just is. We look around at our life and see all the things that aren't fair. We may take on a victim mentality and think that life is doing *to* us. Or we may take on the warrior mentality and know that we can move through all the blocks and obstacles that life throws our way. Either way, the real cause is the underlying paradigm: *Life isn't fair.*

So if *Life isn't fair* is your belief, think of all the unfair circumstances you perceive having occurred in your life. You don't

91

necessarily create unfair circumstances, but difficult or challenging situations will show up in your life that you perceive as unfair. Or you may simply perceive a neutral event as being unfair to you. Life is happening and you are putting your own meaning to it. You call something unfair, while a friend who doesn't have that belief system calls it "just life" with no judgment on it. Notice if this happens. Are you caught in the negative emotions and energy of "unfair" while your friend remains neutral? That's a clue that you have this subconscious limiting belief.

The Positive Intent of "Life Isn't Fair" was for a child to know what to expect in life, and then to choose either to accept it or try to change it. On the one hand, the positive intent could have been to motivate children to create more fairness in their life. At a young age, they may have become very vocal about what seemed not right and fair, and demand equality with their siblings, for instance. On the other hand, this belief could have led children to give in to life and simply accept the inequality, not demand or require it to be fair. Children could have gone either direction with this belief to prepare themselves for life.

"I'M POWERLESS"

The truth is that when we are young children, we are actually quite powerless. We don't have physical size or strength on our side, we're too young to have full reasoning capabilities, and we don't have emotional maturity. Even though we may have felt and actually been powerless as a child, that belief system was never meant to be the blueprint for the rest of our life. It was what happened years ago. It was true then, but not now.

The way our brain works is: When our beliefs, feelings, and physical sensations get recorded, they suspend intact in that moment. Later, whenever that belief, *I am powerless,* is reactivated, the energy of that original situation floods through our mind, body, emotions, chemistry, and we again *feel* absolutely powerless – and we believe we truly *are* powerless. The original event may have happened years ago, but if we have not updated that belief, in our powerlessness, our body experiences it countless times over the ensuing years.

The truth is: You are *not* powerless. Period. Your thinking makes you feel and act powerless, but that doesn't mean you actually *are* powerless. It only means you *feel* and *act* powerless. But, since you are no longer that child, you have the ability to make different choices.

Look at your day and notice all the choices you made, from the moment you woke up until you went to sleep at night. Your day was filled with choices. You have the power to make choices. You chose what to wear, you chose to go to work, you chose what to eat for lunch, you chose how you responded to others throughout the day, and you chose how to spend your evening. Listen inside and see if you are saying to yourself, "NO, I didn't choose any of that. It was all forced. I didn't want to do any of it." Thinking you didn't choose any of it, or knowing you chose it all, either way shows you have the power to choose how you see your life.

I'm powerless is simply two words. It's a thought, two words, filled with energy, emotion, and physical sensations. You believe it to be true and so you live it out, finding yourself in situations and challenges where you can't see a way to be in charge. You believe you are powerless, and when life reflects that back to you, you defend it, you live it.

I'm powerful is also simply two words. For you, however, that statement may lack the emotion and the feeling of truth because you filter that thought through the more emotionally charged negative opposite, *I am powerless*. So it doesn't feel true and you don't live it out. You don't see any options – except to act power-less – in challenging situations.

The Positive Intent of "I'm powerless" was often meant to keep you safe, so that you didn't fight back against the bigger powers in your life, your parents, other adults or older siblings. It was also meant to help you accept being disappointed and not getting your own way. If you knew that you were powerless to make things happen the way you wanted, it wouldn't be such a surprise or hurt as much when that occurred again and again.

As an adult, this belief can lead you into the truth of your internal power because you can get so tired of feeling powerless that you break through that belief. It can motivate you to become the powerful Being that you actually are.

HANGIN' ON FOR DEAR LIFE

The Buddha tells a parable of a man walking a high road who sees a great river, its near bank dangerous and frightening, while its far bank appears safe. The man collects sticks and foliage, makes a raft and paddles across the river, safely reaching the other shore. After reaching the safe shore, he then takes the raft and puts it on his head and walks with it wherever he goes. It's not something he needs, but the raft helped him get across the river, so he hangs onto it.

This parable demonstrates what I've been writing about with all of the positive intents of the limiting beliefs. You can see that we hang onto them because they were originally meant to help us, regardless of the impacts they now have on our adult life. We also hold onto false beliefs because we believed they kept us safe as a child.

Our habitual beliefs also stay in place because they are familiar. We know the world according to our perceptions. So even if these perceptions destroy the quality of our life, we still consider them "comfortable" because we have always lived through them. We may not know who we would be without this way of being, even though we want it to be gone.

We may also hold onto outdated beliefs out of loyalty to our family. For instance, *"I'll be letting my father down by letting go of this belief,"* or *"Something bad will happen to my mother if I speak the truth,"* or *"It's not OK to earn more money or be more successful than my parents."* You may even feel as though you keep someone else alive or happy because of a limiting belief you embrace.

YOU MADE IT ALL UP

Think of all of these limiting beliefs and their opposite empowering beliefs as hungry wolves within you. Which ones will win out and rule you in the moment? That all depends on which ones you feed. You, and you alone, decide which beliefs you will feed and nourish: those that constrict you or those that empower you.

With all the limiting beliefs just discussed and the thousands of others that constrict or empower you, it's important to remember one thing:

You made them all up.

An event occurred. You made up the meaning of the event, you turned it into a belief, and then you generalized it to the rest of your life. The original event was neutral facts – you or someone else said or did something, or something happened. You gave that event meaning. You put judgments on it, and you had thoughts about what that meant about you and others. You were flooded with emotions and feelings. And it all became intertwined and recorded in your brain. You have experienced this belief ever since as though it is the Truth.

That's often a tough pill to swallow, but the good news is:

You can make up something else.

EMPOWERING THOUGHTS

- Originally, we saw each belief as a solution to a problem.

- *I'm not good enough* is a lie, just as are all the other limiting beliefs.

- All beliefs and thoughts can be released or transformed.

- The *only thing* that is actually true is that you have a *belief* that you were abandoned.

- You, the Soul of who you are, are Love. At your core, you are perfect.

- Never ever are the thoughts or perceptions of a three-year-old valid for a person in their thirties, forties, fifties, or older!

- We give meaning to our world through the stories we make up in our minds.

- "If that happens, my God and I will handle it."

- Our journey is to realize that these "less than" beliefs are not true.

- Your thinking makes you feel and act powerless, but that doesn't mean you actually *are* powerless.

PART II

Change Your Thinking

5

Change Your Viewpoint

This is what we all want to know, isn't it? How do we transform our limiting perceptions that are so deeply held and rooted in our subconscious mind? By now you are well aware that they create your unhealthy habits and, essentially, dictate your very way of living life. In so doing, they don't make you happy or successful.

In any moment, you can change a negative, limiting thought to a more empowering one using your conscious mind. If you think, "I can't do that," and you notice this thought, then you can consciously choose to think, "If someone else has done that, then it can be done, and I can do it or learn to do it." The problem is that most of the time we don't even notice we're thinking the negative thoughts. They are just there, habitually in our mind, feeling true.

Here are two vital points about changing your belief systems.

First, and foremost, it's important to remember that most of your subconscious beliefs are working for you, helping you live life in a positive manner. Think of all the little things you know how to do regularly: brush your teeth, get dressed, cook, walk, remember what you learned in school, tell others interesting information you've read, create, participate in sports, share your intellectual knowledge, put together a jigsaw puzzle, drive a car, sing or play a musical instrument, and so on. It's astounding how many beliefs you have that enable you to navigate through each day well.

The number of beliefs that cause you the greatest pain and suffering is nominal compared to your myriad of healthy, helpful beliefs. So take a moment to acknowledge all the ways you are successfully living life. Even in the darkest of times or lowest moments, most of your beliefs work for you, rather than seemingly against you.

Second, know that changing a belief is one of the most natural things we do in life. You have been automatically transforming and upgrading your beliefs your entire life. We all do it, all the time. It's what we all do when we learn something new, and let go of old thinking and perceptions. You learned to walk, which was a huge feat, and then walking became your natural state. The thought of not being able to walk was no longer in your consciousness. Growth and change are your natural states of being. Think how many of your beliefs have changed since you were a child – the large majority of them! Letting go of the old as you step into the new is inbred, hardwired, and simply part of who we all are.

However, some beliefs, patterns, behaviors, and thoughts have not changed, even when we know their source. We can intellectually know why we do something limiting, where that behavior came from, and even do therapy to change it – and still the behavior remains.

Think about making New Year resolutions and how much you intend to keep those changes in the coming year. It is a time when many people join gyms, start diet programs, and seek credit counseling. We all know what we need to do to make those desired changes: exercise more, eat healthier foods, eat fewer unhealthy foods, or spend less money. You start off doing the intended behaviors and, if typical, those behaviors fall by the wayside within about six weeks. What happened to your intentions and desires to make changes? Why don't they continue?

The answer is: The programming in your subconscious mind hasn't changed, so the external behaviors won't change in a lasting way. You can bypass the subconscious programming for a time, but unless something shifts on your subconscious level, at the root cause of the belief, the old habits and behaviors will begin to reappear.

I'm beginning this discussion of transforming your beliefs by describing six ways you might not think are connected to this subject. Rather than starting with therapeutic modalities and different techniques for releasing subconscious blocks, which comes in the next two chapters, I'm starting with a soul-full approach. These are ways of Being that will help you change your life, from the inside out, and assist you in indirectly changing your belief systems. You'll find more of this in Part III, which delves more fully into the soul's perspective.

- Appreciate the Magnetism of Gratitude

- Find the Forgiveness Within You

- Experiment With the Power of Prayer

- Experience the Gift of Grace

- Be in the Present Moment

- Aim for Balance of Heart and Mind

APPRECIATE THE MAGNETISM OF GRATITUDE

The first step in changing your beliefs may very well be gratitude. That's right, be grateful.

Be grateful for all the good that is in your life. Be grateful for who you are and for all your experiences and accomplishments. What you have been through, and what you may be going through now, has made you who you are today...and it is the foundation for who you will become next week, next year, in the next decade.

Gratitude for *everything* in your life is the end-point goal. If you knew, really knew, that your limiting beliefs were your greatest allies toward becoming your greatest self, would you begin to imagine being grateful, really soul-level grateful, for the perceptions that have most limited you? That's hard to imagine, isn't it? Well, perhaps. But when you have gained the consciousness of gratitude, you will find that your limiting perceptions no longer have the power over your life that they used to have. In fact, they've taught you much worth valuing.

Those who cultivate the habit and attitude of being grateful "no matter what" become those who have the most to be grateful for. It's self-fulfilling. If you look for things to be grateful for, even in the midst of chaos, destruction or loss, you *can* find it. You may have to look hard, but there is always something to be grateful for.

If you focus on that, if you give thanks for those gifts in your life, then you will begin to experience more of those gifts. Gratitude is a magnet, just like limiting beliefs. Both attract like. But one attracts more good into your life while the other attracts more not-so-good.

If you want to change your limiting beliefs, begin to dwell on the good that is already in your life, the good that is working for you, and the good that you are creating. Begin to dream and envision what you want and be grateful, in advance, for that appearing in your life.

Caroline Myss, www.myss.com, a wise woman, best-selling author, lecturer, and spiritual teacher, says, "It's easy to be grateful when you're at a banquet. But when it really counts is when the cupboards are bare." You have the power to choose what you focus on.

When you are trying to change some aspect of your life, you tend to focus only on that one area, and so your scope narrows down to a small part of who you are. But that's not *all* that you are. It's not even *who* you are. It's a belief taken on much earlier in life that is loaded with energy and emotion and is replaying over and over, seemingly taking over your life. That's what's behind your anguish about an issue. It can be changed! Take a breath and widen your vision to remember that you are more than those few "problem areas" of your life.

Know this Truth about yourself: You are an Infinite Being with infinite possibilities.

When you're in a dark place, or really stuck in some area of your life, those words can sound like rubbish, hocus pocus, or true for someone else, but not for you. They can even make you angry because they feel so far removed from your current reality. At any moment in time – *any moment* – a shift in your perception can occur and your life suddenly changes. That possibility exists for all of us, equally, at all times.

I know this to be Truth. If you can't or don't believe it, then perhaps you can hang on to my knowing that it is Truth. Recognize that I believe it, know it, and have experienced it. Realize that I know thousands of people who have learned through experience: At any moment in time, you can change your beliefs and perceptions about who you are and your life will change accordingly.

FIND THE FORGIVENESS WITHIN YOU

There are many definitions of forgiveness. *A Course in Miracles* defines it as: a shift in perception that removes a block in me, to my awareness of love's presence. On Oprah Winfrey's television show a few years back, a guest defined forgiveness as: letting go of the hope that the past could be different. Wikipedia.com defines it as "the intentional and voluntary process by which a victim undergoes a change in feelings and attitude regarding an offense, lets go of negative emotions, such as vengefulness, with an increased ability to wish the offender well."

"There is no healing without forgiveness." I've heard this statement about forgiveness through the years and I believe it to be true. All healing requires you to let go of what is causing the disease within you, whether it is physical, emotional, or mental. The major religions of the world include forgiveness as one of their main tenets. It's part of effective therapeutic work. Many self-help books include techniques for forgiving. If you search "forgiveness" online, you'll be rewarded with countless references of all types on this subject.

It makes sense to resist forgiving someone if you believe forgiveness means that you need to: condone or accept what the other person said or did to hurt you; just overlook, accept or pardon; or "be the bigger person" and move on.

But nothing could be further from the truth. First of all, forgiveness is not about – or for – the other person. Forgiveness is only about you. Forgiveness is for you.

We forgive so that we no longer carry the negative emotions, toxic thinking, and hostility toward the other person(s) within us. Non-forgiveness creates resentments within us. We typically replay the harm done to us over and over in our minds, changing the scenarios so that the other person suffers or loses. All the while we are flooding our mind and body with toxic thoughts, chemicals, emotions, and reactions. The saying that so well describes this is: Resentment is like you drinking the poison and hoping the other person will die.

We forgive so that we stop drinking the poison.

We forgive so that we can find inner peace, calm, well being, and love.

We forgive so that we can move on with our life, rather than continuing to be held hostage to something that happened last year or fifty years ago. As long as we continue to hold onto wrongdoings in our mind, the wrongdoing controls us. This is just as true for what we hold against ourselves as for what we hold against others.

Forgiveness isn't just for considerate or benevolent people. We all are born with the ability and the capacity to forgive. It's a conscious choice that we make. Sometimes we need to make this choice to forgive over and over again as we delve deeper and deeper into our negative emotions.

If the hurt happened a while ago, this is what's true: The other person(s) did what they did to you and the actions and behaviors have ended. Every time you replay it in your mind, it is as though you are reliving the hurt. You are re-traumatizing yourself. The other person may have treated you wrongly one time, or a dozen times. But in your mind you have been wronged a thousand times, because you replay it over and over. The other person is no longer the cause of your suffering. Your thoughts and emotions now cause your suffering. You may think of it in terms of being violent against yourself.

When you have forgiven, you no longer have strong negative emotions or feel hurt when someone or some situation touches your "hot button." You change to feeling neutral or even grateful because you realize how that original experience has helped you grow.

If you can't get to this neutrality, if you've tried to let go but find your mind keeps pulling back the old stories, you may ask, "How do I really forgive?" There are many sources of answers. Search the Internet for all the valuable suggestions on how and why to forgive. There are over 330,000 YouTube videos on "how to forgive." Over 11,000 books are listed on amazon.com with the word "forgiveness" in the title. The information is readily available.

Forgiveness is an important aspect of releasing old beliefs because it is your thinking and perceptions that determine: how you view the wrongdoings; why you are hanging onto the negative emotions; what should or shouldn't have occurred; how the other person ought to have behaved; how you might have responded;

and all the other variables that you are holding onto. It is your beliefs that are causing you the grief. You can change your perceptions. Forgiveness is the pathway.

EXPERIMENT WITH THE POWER OF PRAYER

Prayer is also a powerful change agent – far more powerful than you may realize. Whatever you may believe about prayer, I can assure you it's *not* the little rote prayers so many of us were taught as children before bedtime. The prayer I'm talking about is actually meant to heal – us, situations, others, attitudes, lives.

Prayer is communication between you and your Higher Self/ God/Source/Soul/The Almighty/Allah/The Divine/The Great Spirit. For me, prayer can be as simple as just a chat, a talk, with my heart, with my Soul, with Source. Prayer embodies gratitude. At other times, I go inside myself into a deep inner communion with Source. I feel the love deeply and I simply rest in that Presence and Power. I set my ego and busy mind aside and put my attention into feeling the presence of Source within.

Prayer is acknowledging grace or blessings. Prayer is many things, but most of all it is alive, vibrant, and real. It is a powerful creative force in this Universe.

Gregg Braden is a *New York Times* best-selling author, visionary, engaging speaker, amazing teacher, and a true spiritual leader of our times. In his book, *The Divine Matrix,* he writes that the "power" of prayer is in the feeling. It's all about feelings. In bold typeface he states, "Not just any feeling will do. The ones that create must be without ego and judgment."

Prayer has been proven to significantly reduce the crime rate in areas where a small group of people have focused their attention on peace and said positive prayers. The crime rate has been charted before, during, and after such prayer vigils, and, time and again, crime has significantly dropped during the prayers and then begun to rise again after the vigils were over.

In one of the many near death experience books I've read, I remember a description of prayer as streams of light shooting out from earth into the heavens. Some were bright, bold, and full of energy. Some were weak and barely left the earth. There is a difference in the power of prayers. Not all prayers are equal; the strength depends on the heart, mind and feelings of the person praying.

Similarly, Dr. Larry Dossey, in his book *Prayer Is Good Medicine*, writes about scientific studies done to prove the efficacy of prayer. They used grass seeds in different containers with a group of people praying specific prayers for each container. One container was the control group and received no prayer, the second container was prayed to grow, the third was prayed to grow a certain height, and the fourth was prayed for its highest good. The results were statistically significant. All three prayed-for groups grew higher than the control group, and container three grew higher than number two. But the greatest growth was in the fourth container in which the prayer was for the grass seeds' highest good.

We cannot know someone's highest good because we do not know what each person is here to learn and experience. We also do not know their path. So when we pray for others, or even for ourselves, the most powerful prayer is for their (and our) highest good, to be blessed, graced, and loved. To pray for specific outcomes is like praying for containers two and three above to grow, or to grow to a certain height. Such prayers can help, but they are not the most effective or life-changing prayers.

If you pray for highest good, and then you follow the insights, intuitions, and guidance you receive, you can't begin to imagine how your life will change. Unfortunately, what's common in human nature is that you won't follow the guidance you receive because it goes contrary to what you have been doing. That's exactly the point! What you have been doing and thinking has gotten you into the situation you're in. It will take different actions and different thoughts to change your world. Follow your guidance and intuition, but don't confuse them with your fears or fantasies.

There are many types of prayers, two of which are:

- Prayers of supplication

- Prayers of affirmation

Prayers of supplication, also known as petitioning, are the begging and bargaining type, "Please, God, do this for me and I promise I'll…." This is not the most effective way to pray because you are in the consciousness of fear. You see the power of God as outside of yourself, so you need to do something to gain God's approval, or to suddenly and magically have all your ills cured, or problems solved. In this case, you're actually telling God how to do His/Her/Its business. You think you can direct God's will to do what you want done.

Prayers of affirmation, or affirmative prayers, according to Wikipedia.com, are a form of prayer or a metaphysical technique that is focused on a positive outcome rather than on a negative situation. For example, a person who is experiencing some form of illness would focus the prayer on the desired state of perfect health and affirm this desired intention as if it already happened. This is the opposite of identifying the illness and then asking God for help to eliminate it. In affirmative prayer, you *feel* the end

111

result as deeply as you can. Feel and know that highest good is already prevailing. This requires a deep trust in the Infinite, rather than worrying and fretting about the current situation.

For me personally, prayers of supplication are outdated models of who we are and how prayer works. They are prayers *to* the Divine, and are still practiced widely by people of all faiths. But there are other ways of being in prayer *with* the Divine.

If you know, or even hope, that you are part of Source/All That Is, that you are an eternal Spirit, then you know (or hope) the presence, power, and essence of the Divine is within you. Therefore, why are you bargaining? It's not that someone or something is "out there." Rather, it's within you. Source is within you, expressing through you, as you. You may not be able to believe this fully, but if you begin to try this on, to sit with it, to pray about it, your own truth can be revealed to you.

Find your own knowing about Source, the Divine, especially if what you have been taught or read doesn't resonate with the deepest part of you. Trust yourself and follow your path to your experience of the Divine. Start with your breath. Follow your breath inside, into the silence within.

When you pray, see if you can go inside and connect with your heart, with Source within you, with the Love that is within you. This takes you out of fear consciousness and into Love consciousness. From there, when you pray for highest good, you are affirming and coming into alignment with Source. It's quite different from begging and bargaining. This praying is based in Love and expectation that all we need is already provided.

What does this have to do with changing limiting belief systems? For instance, if you are filled with resentment because of something that has been done to you, what if you begin to pray for those who harmed you? What if you pray for their highest good? Does that go against everything you want to do? Or does that resonate deeply with you as a positive step you can take to move beyond your resentment? In praying for their highest good, you will begin to feel peace and calm within yourself.

The Alcoholics Anonymous program teaches a 21-day prayer process that I personally know changes lives and relationships. In addition to my own experiences with it, I have had numerous clients use this process and report back remarkable changes. It's quite simple, but not always easy to follow.

For 21 days, you pray for the person you have animosity toward, or are in a strained relationship with, or hold a grudge against. Whomever you see as a problem in your life, begin to pray for their highest good. Pray that they be blessed, abundant, and all good comes to them. Keep it general, rather than list specific outcomes. You don't have to mean it, just pray it. In fact, you may not mean it at all in the beginning. But if you keep praying for them every single day, you will change. You will begin to mean it. If you skip a day, go back and start the 21-day cycle over again.

Do you really want to change the relationship and how you feel about the other person? Do you really want peace of mind within yourself? If so, do this practice. If all you want to do, deep inside, is complain about that person, then carry on with your complaining. It's your choice.

What *you feel* inside is not about the other person. It's all about you. It's your own perceptions, beliefs, and wounds that are being retriggered from earlier in life. Now you have the power within you to change that. Rather than focus on the other person's behaviors, which absolutely may be unacceptable, you keep your attention on your own reactions. You can do something about your own reactions. This is where your power lies. This is where change occurs.

Prayer changes us, perhaps more than anyone we are praying for. The act of praying, of going inside and connecting with our heart and divine nature, can transform beliefs and cast out untruths. If you don't know how to pray, begin by getting quiet, close your eyes, breathe, and tell the truth. "Teach me to pray. I don't know how to pray." Then sit quietly and listen. Stop talking in your head; just listen. If you don't hear anything, give thanks anyway. As you do this daily practice, you *will* begin to hear your inner voice. When you do, it's up to you to follow the guidance however it may show up. Your prayer of how to pray will be answered, although perhaps not in the way you expect.

Another very powerful heart-opening prayer practice is the Hawaiian practice of Ho'noponopono, described by Dr. Joe Vitale in his book *Zero Limits* (as well as by numerous other practitioners). You can find many references on the Internet. The beauty of this practice is its simplicity. The term Ho'noponopono means, "to make right," because it is a practice of reconciliation and forgiveness.

The basis of this work is that you are 100% responsible for everything that comes into your life. If there is someone, or something, in your life that is upsetting, then you take responsibility for bringing it into your life. If the other person has some quality you dislike, find that same quality within yourself and be willing to release it. If this work calls to you, please delve into it further, and make it part of your daily life.

To say this prayer, put yourself into a quiet meditative space, breathe a few times deeply, and bring to mind the person with whom you want to have more harmony. Be willing to release all the stories you tell yourself about that person. Get your ego out of your way. Stop being right for a moment. Just be present. You then repeat these four phrases in your mind and heart, sinking ever deeper into your heart. If you feel called to change the order of these phrases, then do so.

1. I'm sorry.

2. Please forgive me.

3. Thank you.

4. I love you.

If you start to yawn while saying this prayer, know that you are simply releasing negative energy stored inside you. The prayer is working in you. If you get weepy, know that the prayer is working in you. Keep saying the prayer until you feel complete. As simple as this prayer is, it is still very powerful. It is Soul work. You can also make this prayer even more powerful by saying it out loud. You don't need to say it to anyone. Simply hearing yourself say it can deepen its value to you. Experiment to see what works for you.

EXPERIENCE THE GIFT OF GRACE

Grace is one of my favorite qualities of the Divine. I think that grace is like the air we breathe. It is always flowing in, around, and through us. We cannot escape its presence. We're often not aware of it until we put our attention on it. The more we open up to it, and the more we are aware of grace, the more we are able to partake of its blessings.

Arianna Huffington, in her book *Thrive: The Third Metric to Redefining Success and Creating a Life of Well-Being, Wisdom, and Wonder*, quotes John-Roger, the founder of the Movement of Spiritual Inner Awareness: "Grace isn't something that you go for, as much as it's something you allow. However you may not know grace is present, because you have conditioned the way you want it to come, for example, like thunder or lightning, with all the drama, rumbling, and pretense of that. In fact, grace comes in very naturally, like breathing."

When you become aware of grace, you may feel a sense of being deeply loved, or you may feel that all is in divine right order, or you may have a sense of well being. Often I feel a warm sensation, along with a feeling of being loved, in my heart area. What you are feeling is the presence of the Divine – the grace of the Divine – the Divine's gift to us.

In this moment right now, close your eyes and take a conscious breath in and out. Stop for just a moment. Simply ask for grace or become aware of it surrounding you, and breathe it in. Let it move through you. Notice what you're noticing. I sink deeper into gratitude as I feel the presence of the Divine move through my body in the form of grace.

If you feel nothing, keep practicing, keep asking for grace, and you may notice it in a very different manner. Perhaps, when you least expect it, you will be filled with a sense of well being, that all is taken care of, that you are deeply loved. Or you may feel grace when you are in nature, breathing in the beauty of all that surrounds you, feeling connected and in oneness with nature.

However you experience it, whatever you call it, know that it is real and present, and available to you at all times. We can block ourselves from feeling grace but that doesn't mean it's not there – still flowing through us.

If you have no sense of it at all, then just pretend. It's OK to pretend if that's where you need to start. It's real and it can become real for you. In the meantime, act as if there's this thing called grace, and when you put your attention on it, it fills you. Just imagine what that might feel like. Act as if it's real. You may need to prime the pump some, imagining, pretending. Know this, however, that grace is very real and can indeed fill your heart, mind, and Soul. It's surrounding you now, ready to be made aware of and asked to enter in.

Once you are aware of grace, you can enter into prayer or gratitude, or simply go on about your day, checking back in to notice that grace is remaining with you.

How does this practice help you to change your limiting beliefs? Bring one of your chronic limiting beliefs to mind, feeling it vividly in your body. Now breathe into grace, giving your attention to the presence of the Divine. Notice what happens. I don't know about you, but I experience a deep love inside that causes the limiting belief to lose its power or intensity. This practice can instantly move you into a different consciousness from that of the limiting belief, thereby creating a shift inside. The more you move your attention from that which limits you to that which empowers you, the more you live an empowered life.

BREATHE INTO THE PRESENT MOMENT

One way to "unfreeze" yourself, so that you can release an old limiting belief and take on a new empowering one, is to bring yourself into the present moment. Here's an example of doing that when feeling "powerless." If powerlessness is not one of your limiting beliefs, just choose another word for a feeling that limits you.

Every time you notice yourself thinking or feeling, *"I'm powerless,"* stop in that moment and take a deep and conscious breath. Feel your breath! If you don't feel it, breathe again and notice your intake and outflow of breath.

Your breath is vitally important in helping you change your energy because, when you notice it and focus on it, it brings you into the present moment.

Your feeling of being powerless is not rooted in the present moment. It's habitual thinking from the past. Breathe deeply and come into the present moment. Notice your body, pat yourself, and feel the sensations of your hands on your body. Sometimes I lightly tap my face and my third eye in the center of my forehead, breathing and telling myself, "Be here now!"

When you are present in the moment, tell yourself the truth, such as: *"That's an old thought and it's not true for me now. I am not that child any longer. I am powerful. I am safe. I am able to change my world."*

Then bring to mind memories of when you have been powerful, when you have felt safe, and when you have changed your world. Feel those positive memories strongly, filling your body with their invigorating energy.

Get into the feeling! That's very important because our feeling self gives us the key to uncovering our limiting beliefs. Let these positive memories and feelings fill your mind and body. Focus on them intently. Again, pull up these memories of when you have felt powerful, safe, and experienced changing your world. Bring these memories into your conscious mind because that's where you can focus on them. So find them! Feel them! Relive them, vividly.

Do this whenever you encounter moments of stress. *Switch your attention from what you don't want to what you do want.*

If your mind wants to pull you back into feeling powerless, breathe deeply again and repeat the process of reminding yourself about when you have felt powerful. Energize the thought *"I am powerful, I am safe."*

You *can* change your thinking. You can begin to drain out the negative energy of *"I'm powerless"* and convert it into the positive energy of *"I'm powerful."* You can bring these two mindsets into balance within yourself. But it takes more than doing this once or twice, or even staying present to this powerful feeling for a few days or weeks.

Switching from powerless to powerful in your mind needs to become habitual – until you find that the powerless thought has become so totally weakened from its lack of being fed by you that it is no longer active in your thinking. You'll simply begin living from the concept of having the power to make choices that you want to make.

AIM FOR BALANCE OF HEART AND MIND

As you are deeply examining your beliefs and using techniques to change how you show up in life, you may find yourself over-analyzing your life or being swept away by your emotions.

Remember this: aim for balance in all areas of your life. We are built to use both our logical head-mind and our intuitive heart-mind. If either rules too much, we get off balance and our life doesn't run as smoothly as we'd like.

- Our logical mind loves to analyze and be rational. So it focuses on day-to-day business, finances, and worldly success. It's about "doing."

- Our heart-mind takes an intuitive view of circumstances. So it focuses on relationships, intimacy, health, and joy. It's about "being."

The pendulum of learning tends to swing between the two – from one extreme to the other until it comes to rest in the middle ground. It's likely that your default is more to one or the other, and that's what you use in times of stress or when you "go unconscious" – so as not to feel anything in the present moment.

If you follow your heart to an extreme, ignoring your logical mind, you may find the business, financial, and worldly success aspects of life elude you. If you filter your experiences through your logical, analytical, rational mind, then close relationships, intimacy, joy, and the experience of thoroughly loving life in the present moment may elude you. Neither way of being is better or worse, right or wrong, good or bad. Both are necessary, in balance, for a truly well rounded, successful life. It all depends on your beliefs about who you are and how you make decisions.

How close to the balanced middle does your pendulum swing?

If you're a successful Type A driven personality, you may use your intuitive knowing in conjunction with your logical mind to make decisions and see what needs to be done, as well as intuitively feel the right direction to go.

This combination works very well in business and success. In fact, studies have shown that highly successful people follow their intuition rather than their logical mind when faced with a major decision where their logical and intuitive minds disagree. In the same circumstances, less successful people follow their logic, ignoring their intuition. The more successful people have done their homework and use their logical mind to analyze all the data; then they choose to follow their knowing, their gut instinct.

Yet, at home or in their close relationships, these same successful business people may stay more in their logical mind, not opening up to deep intimacy or to experiencing real joy or a sense of peace and contentment in life.

I was in a conference recently where several highly successful people talked about "having it all" in life. Yet, they said they formerly felt that something had been missing that they couldn't quite put their finger on. They then explained that the previous year, while attending the DreamBuilder LIVE conference with Mary Morrissey, they had learned about following their heart, and doing what they loved. They said those two insights made all the difference in their world. They have continued in their same businesses, homes, and families, but they have added elements of what they love. They talked about getting clear on their heart's desires, and for each of them, that included being of service to others by using their success to help others improve the quality of their lives. These successful people had become happier over the intervening year, which meant their pendulum was swinging closer to the middle, by following both their heart and their mind.

What happens if you always follow your heart, do what you love, be of service, help others, put others first, and self-sacrifice? It's likely you're not taking good care of your finances or business, or other aspects that require analytical thinking. It may be that you're well loved and highly regarded, and truly a beacon of light, but there's something elusive missing. What about taking care of your own needs, not just your finances but also your time and energy? What do you do simply for yourself? How well do you take care of yourself? Are you too busy, seemingly not interested, or feel guilty or even driven away from having prosperous finances, a healthy body, and time for your own enjoyment?

None of this is good or bad. I'm talking about balance. Look at your life from the perspective of your underlying beliefs that lead you to repeat unhealthy behaviors and thoughts. Yes, you will have a predisposition to be more analytical or intuitive, but it's then up to you to fill in the other side, to learn to come into balance. Notice how balanced you are in your business, family, love, time, energy, enjoyment, social relationships, and health. You may see balance in some areas, but lack of balance in others.

You know how to be in balance. It's your underlying beliefs that drive you in one direction or another. They actually cause you to believe that they *are* you. But they're not. *You are not your beliefs.* From now on, anytime you say, "This is just how I am," stop and correct yourself. Remember that you are more accurate if you say, "This is how my underlying beliefs make me feel and act."

Here's the overarching Truth: *There is nothing at all wrong with you!* There is nothing to be fixed. You just have feelings, emotions, beliefs, and patterns that are not aligned with feeling good about yourself and achieving the life you desire.

My best piece of advice: Love yourself enough to seek to transform your beliefs, no matter what it takes, and then love yourself through your transformation process! This book will help guide you.

EMPOWERING THOUGHTS

- In any moment, you can change a negative, limiting thought to a more empowering one using your conscious mind.

- Those who cultivate the habit and attitude of being grateful "no matter what" become those who have the most to be grateful for.

- We forgive so that we stop drinking the poison.

- Prayer is many things, but most of all it is alive, vibrant, and real.

- Switch your attention from what you don't want to what you do want.

6

Change Your Story

Let's look at some of these core issues from another viewpoint.

Look at the patterns and issues in your life that you believe are true. You live them out and experience them, so, of course, they seem true. I'd like you to begin to step back and realize something else.

The only thing that is actually true is this: You have *beliefs* that create your experiences. These beliefs are not necessarily true, even though you think they are. What is true is that *you have beliefs* about their being true.

Earlier I gave the example of a mother shopping in the grocery store who went into the next aisle. Her young son was so engrossed in looking at something on the shelves that he didn't realize she was gone until he looked up. He then panicked, fearing that she had left him. That started his lifelong struggle with women leaving him.

The story he told himself was that his mother left him. Here's the truth: His mother did not leave or abandon her son. She simply went into the next aisle. Even at his young age of three, he chose his thoughts about that event. And, as he aged, he continued to choose that story as his truth.

Here's another point: Even if it had been true in that moment – that she had truly "left or abandoned" him – his thought that *"women leave me"* was never supposed to generalize to all female love relationships for the rest of his life. It was a moment in time at age three. That's all it was. It was not the blueprint for how all women would treat him.

No thoughts or perceptions of a three-year-old are valid for people in their forties. The thinking of a child is appropriate for the child, but it is not appropriate or true for the adult simply because it is a *child's* thinking. What you thought in childhood should not be running your life today.

What if you are convinced that your parent actually *did* abandon you as a child?

Even if a parent actually left the home and was gone from the child's daily life, that doesn't mean the parent abandoned the child. It sure looks that way, doesn't it? But what's actually true is that the parent left, or divorced, or died, or moved away. Or more likely, the parent left for work for the day!

OBSERVE YOUR SITUATION OBJECTIVELY

In order to move on from these stories, and the stronghold our beliefs have on our life, we need to look at what actually happened, not what we keep telling ourselves happened. There is often quite a difference.

What's the actual action that occurred? Take the example of parents leaving for work. This action can be traumatic for a young child. Imagine you are that child. You may perceive this situation as *"they are leaving me alone"*. You beg your parents to stay ... but they still go away. You're too young to understand why they are leaving, even though they explain where they are going. You only understand, *You are leaving me!* In that moment when you form that belief, nothing else matters – even if there's a babysitter or your older siblings in the house. Your thoughts and feelings of being abandoned and feeling utterly alone become locked in. In fact, you may even extend that belief to feeling as though you can't trust your parents to *ever* be there for you or fulfill you needs. You form the belief: *"It doesn't matter what I want, they leave me."*

All of this can be the root of a lifelong struggle with feeling abandoned, mistrusting others, and believing your needs are not being met. You, the child, may even decide in that moment that the reason your parents are leaving is because you are not good enough. In short, you turn the belief around, against yourself.

It's a *child's perspective* that becomes rooted in the subconscious. None of it is based in truth, although it feels true to the child. This skewed thinking becomes our reality and we then live it out over and over.

In reality, to say the parent abandoned the child is to change the event of *leaving*, which is what the parent actually did, to a judgment about what the child felt, *abandoned*.

If abandonment is an issue for you, you can now change the story to an adult viewpoint. You can now say, "They left." "They moved." Or "They died." This change improves the story by making it about *them*, not about *you*. As adults, we know that our parents did what they did because of their own wounds or needs or life changes. Their actions weren't against you; their actions were about them.

Changing this story not only gets you, the child, out of the picture, it also states the parent's action in terms of a fact, rather than as a judgment made by you, the child.

I've had many clients who talk about having been emotionally abandoned. *"My mother wasn't there for me emotionally."* If this is you, I bet you, too, can cite all the times you needed her and she wasn't available. What you say may very well have been true. And you may have been over and over this issue in therapy, and still the pain and emptiness remain. In fact, you likely may say, "My story is different. It *is true* that my mother abandoned me emotionally!"

Even if this is the case, as you change your story about being abandoned, you will begin to feel a sense of spaciousness around you and healing within you. If your story of being abandoned is painful at this point in your life, it's time to look at your childhood or the other abandonment events from a new perspective – so that you can finally let them go and move on.

Begin by looking at the event from an objective viewpoint. Write down your answers to:

1. What *actually* happened? What did the other person do *for* him/herself rather than *against* you?

2. What within you continues to attract these circumstances into your life?

3. On the bigger Soul-level picture, what are you trying to learn? What is the benefit to you of this event? Who have you become because of the beliefs you formed?

If you have a multitude of people who have left you, it's likely you read this section and say, "Yeah, sure, that's easier said than done. I really have been abandoned! It is true for me!"

Know that our beliefs always seem true to us because when formed, each belief felt true. That feeling of truth has intertwined as part of our belief system so that when a belief is triggered again, the "truth" of it is again experienced in the same way as it first was. Plus, to add fuel to the fire, you have lived through this pattern numerous times, so your life experience also adds to the seeming "truth" of the belief.

The best thing you can do for yourself right now is to take a deep breath, slowly let it out, and write your answers. Notice if any of this writing triggers you – that is, gives you a jolt, causes a tear or a shiver, or starts you crying uncontrollably. If you have a response, emotionally or verbally, congratulations! You've just hit upon an issue and its energized beliefs that you can now change for the better.

FORGIVE YOURSELF

The next action is to forgive yourself for any and all stories you've been holding onto. We all do it. We all have our stories of what happened to us, and who did what to us, and why we are the way we are. That's our humanness. Part of our path of learning and growing into a higher consciousness is to more and more quickly forgive others and ourselves for what we have created in our life, for what has happened to us, and for the perceived harm that has been done to us.

In any given moment, you are 100% responsible for the story you are telling yourself. It is *your* story, even if it looks like it's about someone else's fault. It is always your choice what you make an event mean to you. You and you alone are giving meaning to what happens in your life. It's in your head. You are making up the story, and you can rewrite it any time you want.

CHANGING MY STORY

Now that my mother has passed on, I can tell this story. I wouldn't have wanted her to know that what I told myself for most of my life was, *"My mother is not here for me emotionally."* I believed this, I felt this loss, and I didn't talk about it with her or others, other than in therapy. I now realize that my not talking about it was a disservice to both her and me. Had I discussed this with her while she was alive, we both could have grown in consciousness, because she could have owned her behaviors and I could have owned mine. We might have grown much closer from my speaking up; but it never happened.

A few years before she died, I did have a heart-to-heart talk with *myself* about this story I was telling myself about her. The gist of it went like this:

"What would my mother say in response to me telling her she wasn't emotionally available to me?"

I looked at it from her viewpoint, not from mine, and I realized she would have been horrified and heartbroken to know I had kept this mindset throughout my life. It wasn't her truth at all. She felt that being a mother was the most important thing in the world – and that she had done her best.

I asked myself: Is this a story I'm telling myself about how she is?

The answer: Of course it's a story; it's all a story. Was she perfect? Was this her strong suit? Absolutely not.

Does that mean she wasn't available .... or ... was it that I withdrew?

Ooohhhh... bringing it back to myself. I had to own my part in our relationship.

I withdrew and told myself she wasn't there for me. I could see all the countless times she had absolutely been on my side. And I could see how I withdrew or didn't reach out to her.

That's when the shift happened: When I consciously chose to tell myself that my mother really *was* there for me emotionally. I acknowledged that I'd been telling myself a "negative" story, and now I chose to tell myself a "positive" story. I no longer wanted to be held hostage to my old story.

Amazing things happened once I owned my story. I don't think my mother changed at all, but I began to feel emotionally supported by her. And, by the way, I know she had been that way all along – to the best of her ability. I forgave myself for having told that story to myself for so long.

What I had been telling myself about our relationship was all in my head, and I had the control to change that.

CHANGE YOUR STORY

You may actually have a parent, spouse, friend, child, boss, or sibling who is not emotionally available to you. "That's just how our relationship is," you may say. If you would like to change that, why not use the same process I used?

See the relationship from their point of view. Pretend to be them. Answer your questions as you think they would answer them. It's called role-playing. You know them well enough that you know what they are likely to say.

Next, describe your actions in the relationship. Like me, you are likely to realize the large role you play in that relationship.

Then notice if and how your relationship changes. The other person may or may not change. Even if nothing changes in *their* behavior, you will find healing in yourself because *you change* when you acknowledge your part in the relationship, the beliefs you've held, and the actions you've taken.

Your relationship will change because you will respond to that person differently. Your tone of voice changes when you talk to them. Your body language changes when you are around them. Your feelings about them change. And when all these subtle, yet important, changes happen, you view the other person in a very different light. You see them more objectively, perhaps even more "Divine-like."

The pain won't be as great because you won't have the same expectations of that person. As you let go of your own childhood wounding, you come into a more centered and grounded relationship within yourself, which is called peace.

It's your path to let go of your stories that lead you to feel upset, guilty, stressed, angry, resentful, envious, manipulated, unsupported, or any other negative emotion. It's time for you to change your story, heal, and move on in your life.

HEALING IS NEVER ABOUT THE OTHER PERSON

I had a female client who was continually upset by her sister. She had done enough therapy work to know that her upset wasn't really about her sister's behavior; it was her own emotion-packed belief system about her sister's actions that upset her. This isn't to say that her sister's behaviors and actions were acceptable. No, they were not. But this was just how her sister was. The upset was entirely within my client.

At the beginning of one session she said, "I know it's usually my stuff, but this time I just know it's my sister and not me!" At the end of the session she said, "I can't believe that was all my stuff. It looked so much like it was all her!"

As an adult, healing is *never* about the other person. It looks like it's about the other person. You'd like it to be about the other person because that relieves you of responsibility. But – take a deep breath – it is *always* all about you and your perceptions.

STAYING A VICTIM IS YOUR CHOICE

I had a wise teacher, Jason Shulman, who taught us that "all wounding happens in relationship, and all healing happens in relationship."

Many people have suffered greatly at the hands of others. It's real, it actually happens, and it's not just a belief we have. We are hurt, wounded, beaten, and victimized by others. Victimization is insidious in the ways it grows out of hand and has such far reaching rippling and crippling effects.

If you were abused in any way whatsoever when you were young, it wasn't your fault. It doesn't matter what the abuser told you or how you came to believe that you caused it. The one who victimizes is at fault. This goes for sexual, physical, mental, and emotional abuse, including bullying. The perpetrator is the aggressor and therefore at fault.

As you've aged, you may have suffered in countless ways because of early abuse. Being abused or victimized can deeply affect your sense of self, causing you to feel worthless, dirty, guilty, unloved, unlovable, shamed, bad, invisible, insignificant, and countless other aspects of disrespect. You may have held yourself back from succeeding, you may have eating disorders, alcoholism, drug abuse, failed relationships, financial hardships, and other obstacles that are in your way of being happy, successful, and feeling right inside yourself.

No matter what has happened to you, no matter in what ways you have been victimized or abused, your *mindset* of thinking of yourself as a victim is your choice. Being victimized is not always a choice; being a victim is a choice. Just because you were victimized, that doesn't make you a victim. Victim is a way of thinking about yourself. It's not the same as the action of being victimized.

There are people who have undergone brutality that horrifies the imagination. The cruelty or tragic life situations they have experienced shouldn't happen to anyone. Their path of healing is to move away from thinking of themselves as victims. That's how complete healing happens. You can still have unfortunate events and actions that seem to be against you in life, but it's how you respond that determines if you see yourself as a victim or not.

Part of the healing in moving out of being a victim is to tell your story of what somebody did to you or against you. We all need to be heard. Our story needs to be acknowledged. This is what 12-step work and counseling are all about. That's how we heal. We tell our story and we are heard.

There comes a time, however, when you need to let go of the story and move into a deeper level of healing where you take responsibility for your subconscious beliefs that continue to perpetuate the victimization or that contribute to your not letting go of your wounding.

All wounding is meant to heal. Wounding and healing are part of the same spectrum; they co-exist. Just as a physical wound naturally heals with time, so too are mental and emotional wounds within us supposed to heal. So what gets in the way of that healing? *We* get in the way!

If you continue to live in the same mentality and consciousness, repeating your story to yourself and others for years on end, it's like you're ripping a bandage off a physical wound and pouring dirt and grime into it. You keep re-infecting yourself with the dirt and grime of disrespectful and unloving energy. You keep re-energizing with negativity.

At some point – and only you can determine when that point is – it's time to take responsibility for your inner world. While it may seem like healing is about the other person, in truth, your healing has nothing to do with others or what they have done to you. Rather, it's all about what you perceived about what they said or did, and how and why you have held onto that perception for years on end.

The beliefs we have are of our own creation. Yes, the behaviors of others, especially those we give authority to, have a large impact on what we create as our beliefs. *But* – and this is a big but – we are still responsible as adults for the perceptions we have hung onto. An action by a parent thirty years ago that caused some crippling belief system is no longer about that parent. It's now about you acknowledging you are the one who has been hanging onto these beliefs for so long. You were innocent as a child when you formed these beliefs. How can a three-year-old be anything other than innocent for a momentary panic and fear that's natural and age-appropriate?

The responsibility for changing our thoughts and behaviors comes as we age, and we realize that some aspects of our life aren't working well. A young child in elementary school learns she isn't allowed to interrupt the teacher to get attention. This action may come from being the youngest of several children in a noisy household with overwhelmed parents. She learns early on that the way to get attention is to be loud; otherwise, she's overlooked at home. In school, she learns that's not appropriate or allowed, and as her behavior changes, her beliefs change. She's already learning there are different rules for home, school, stores, restaurants, church, etc.

The same holds true for adults. We look at our lives to see what's not working for us and then we take responsibility for changing it, even when it looks like it's the other person's fault. To continually blame others for your misfortune keeps you a victim, with its negative-energy consciousness. You vibrate out into the Universe the thoughts, energies, and emotions of a victim, and that can (and most likely will) attract more victimization in one form or another back to you.

The way out of victimization is to change your story of being a victim. But how do you change the story of what actually happened to you? Keep reading.

EMPOWERING THOUGHTS

- What you thought in childhood should not be running your life today.

- It's a *child's perspective* that becomes rooted in the subconscious. None of it is based in truth, although it feels true to the child.

- You are making up the story, and you can rewrite it any time you want.

- Victim is a way of thinking about yourself. It's not the same as the action of being victimized.

- At some point – and only you can determine when that point is – it's time to take responsibility for your inner world.

7

Change Your Mind

"*No problem can be solved from the same level of consciousness that created it.*" Albert Einstein

When you find aspects of your life that are not working for you, and you want to transform your life, stepping into a new way of acting, being, feeling, and creating based on new patterns of thinking, what do you do? If you've done everything you know how to do on your own, and still the limiting beliefs remain, you may need help from other sources.

UNCOVER AND RELEASE
THE ROOT CAUSE

I use hypnosis to help my clients change their beliefs because it puts them into their subconscious mind, which is where their beliefs can be changed.

I have a free gift for you. If you've made it this far through the book, you deserve a reward! I've created a hypnosis session that you can download for free on my web site, www.NancyCanning. com/store. It's the "Change A Belief" CD in the Store, under the section entitled "CDs." It is clearly marked. The coupon code for the free download is **TRANSFORM,** as in uncover and transform the root cause.

This download takes you back to the root cause of any limiting belief you want to transform. You can use it over and over for different beliefs. Since it is hypnosis, don't ever use it in the car because it will take your attention – or the driver's attention – away from driving!

By now you've learned how beliefs are formed and how to recognize them, so it will be much easier for you to understand the mechanics of releasing them. Since they are held in place by your mind thinking you are still that same age as when you took on the belief, you can go back into that moment of inception and change the original thinking. It can't be done by the logical mind just thinking about it. You need to be in a subconscious state.

Some people get scared at the thought of being hypnotized because they have seen stage shows or movies depicting people being controlled by the hypnotist and doing outrageous things they won't want to do. That's entertainment. That's *not* how hypnosis for healing works. I go into more detail about hypnosis and my sessions in Part IV.

"I'VE REALLY HAD ENOUGH!"

If you're sick and tired of a pattern of behavior, and you've done everything you can think of to change it, sometimes it helps to just plain get angry at it. There can be a moment in time when you go deep within and tell yourself, *"I've had enough!"*

This is much like a mother telling her child to pick up his toys and the child ignores her because there's no real conviction in her voice. She's just saying the words and the child can sense her lack of conviction. This scene can repeat several times until the mother snaps inside, something in her voice and energy changes, and the child obeys and picks up his toys. The mother can be frustrated that it took so long. Why didn't he just obey at the beginning?

Why? Because, up until that point, his mother had not decided, *"Do this now."* It took a change in her energy, inside of herself, before her son felt her conviction. The power of conviction, of saying *"Enough!"* can't be overstated.

Since beliefs are often created in times of high emotions, we can un-create them using high emotions. Back in my mid 30s, I was working as a temporary office worker in different office settings. I considered it a fun challenge to see how quickly I could learn new systems, meet new people, and have the freedom to take time off. I was working towards my PhD in psychology at the time, so I knew how to answer phones.

In one office, I worked for a highly abrasive and negative man. His energy was so demeaning and demanding that I found myself unable to think clearly. I could barely answer the phones correctly. It was so terrible being around him that at lunch on the first day, I sat in my car and screamed and raged at the Universe. I remember screaming – fully meaning every single word to the core of my

Being: *"I WILL NEVER WORK FOR AN ASSHOLE AGAIN!"* I was letting the Universe know, in no uncertain terms, what I intended for myself. Through the intensity of my anger and my absolute resolve, I created a new reality for myself.

I left that temp job within a day and since then I have only worked for and with great people. I just don't run into many rude people, and never are they in my work.

It's not the anger that will change beliefs, though. It's the resolve within you. There is a shift inside that says *"ENOUGH!"* You may have said this before, countless times, but until there is a subtle, yet vital, shift inside *you* that leaves no room for debate, the old beliefs can stay. It's like the mother who says, "pick up your toys" over and over with no results. She hasn't shifted into the consciousness of *"This is how it's going to be!"*

I know this: You have the innate ability to resolve something within you and to make it happen. We all do. It's part of our innate ability as a human.

There's a moment in time when you go inside and clearly tell yourself, *"This is how it's going to be."* You can achieve this resolve by joining forces with your Soul self. That is, you set a clear intention. It's not your mind that does this work. It comes from deeper within you. There's no begging or pleading involved. It's simply a decision you make from deep, deep inside. You are deciding for yourself how you will be, leaving no room for comments or negotiations from your logical mind. Fear will show up and try to lead you back to the old way of being. So you may have to come back to this place of resolve over and over, until your intention is firmly in place within. But each time you return there, it gets easier to take actions from that consciousness.

142

I have had food addiction and weight problems since I was ten years old. It's part of my learning in this lifetime. I've lost track how many times I have said, *"Enough!"* regarding my weight. And then, when I was 49, about five months before turning 50, I had that moment of resolve inside myself. I remember it clearly. I had a different intention: *"I'm going to be my normal weight when I'm 50."* I could feel the shift and the new intention click into place. I had about 60 pounds to lose.

Five months after this shift, I was no closer to my normal weight than before. My birthday came and went and the same old behaviors stayed in place. That summer I was warned that diabetes was just around the corner for me if I didn't change my eating and get off all the sugar. A few months later, I went with a friend to a 12-step meeting for food addiction. This was a new world for me, as I had never been part of recovery work. Long story short, I joined the program, changed my eating, and the weight started to fall off. On the very last day of being age 50, the day before my 51st birthday, I was my desired weight. That resolve within me had taken 17 months, but it happened while I was still 50! (You see, you need to be very specific in your wording because the Universe is paying close attention!)

Since then my weight has gone up and down some, but the "really big battles" with food have subsided. Now I just need to be mindful. I have continued to work with the underlying emotions and beliefs to clear away all the wounds inside that lead to addictive eating. And most recently, I found deeper resolution from a process I'll describe next.

SEEK OUT A TEACHER WHO SPEAKS TO YOUR SOUL

There are people in the world who have come into this life to make a significant difference in the lives of others, sometimes millions of people, teaching them how to improve their health and well being. It's not uncommon for these teachers to have experienced very difficult health challenges and obstacles that they overcame. In learning how to heal themselves and overcome their difficulties, they became passionate and dedicated to finding ways to lead others into healing as well.

Two such amazing teachers are Dr. John Demartini and Dr. Joe Dispenza. While they are both totally dedicated to helping create profound changes in the lives of countless people, and both are chiropractors who have expanded their expertise far beyond their initial training, they have very different approaches to healing.

I'll describe their work briefly here and recommend you visit their web sites.

REALIZE THAT YOUR "GOOD" AND "BAD" BALANCE PERFECTLY

Dr. John F. Demartini (www.drdemartini.com) began his career as a doctor of chiropractic and then went on to explore more than 200 different disciplines in pursuit of what he calls Universal Principles of Life and Health. In his 2002 book, *The Breakthrough Experience,* he describes the need to balance all aspects of our lives. He teaches that through balancing our opposites, we can achieve equilibrium and can move through life freed from the mental burdens and wounds we carry from calling something "good" or "bad."

The Demartini Method® developed by Dr. John Demartini is a scientific process that balances perceptions and emotions. It is being used professionally by many psychologists, psychiatrists, social workers, educators, consultants and health professionals across the world. The Demartini Method® is a tool with a thousand uses for empowering and inspiring life and its applications include reducing stress, resolving conflict and creating new perspectives and paradigms for life.

He writes, "The Demartini Process® is the most powerful tool I've found for dissolving illusions, centering the mind, opening the heart, and awakening inner vision and genius."

If you haven't experienced it for yourself, those may just be nice words. But once you've gone through the process, you know that his description is absolutely what happens within you. You can turn the worst thing that has ever happened to you into an event for which you now have immense gratitude. If I hadn't done this work, I'm quite sure I would be skeptical of such high and mighty claims. But I found them to be true.

Dr. Demartini's work brings your conflicts and "issues," as well as your fantasies and expectations, into equilibrium. His work balances both sides of any issue you may have. He believes that for every challenge you face, you receive an equal amount of support. Likewise, for every "fantasy or infatuation," there is a "nightmare" of equal intensity. If you put someone on a pedestal, or have an infatuation with some aspect of another's life, then you suffer because you believe you don't have that human characteristic inside yourself. Your suffering is your nightmare.

On the other hand, if you dislike a quality or trait in another, finding fault or disgust with that person, you suffer from that judgment. In his work, you can take any trait you see in another, or in yourself, and through a process of seeking answers inside yourself, you balance the trait with its opposite trait. The outcome is a deep sense of inner peace, equanimity, and love. That trait in yourself, and in others, loses its intensity as you see it holistically – in balance.

For instance, if you see yourself as fearful while seeing someone else as fearless, then you may admire that trait in them. In doing this work with a friend, she was expecting to start off by listing all the ways she was fear*ful*, because that's how she thought of herself. She was quite surprised when I began, "Tell me all the ways you are fear*less*." As we talked, she found more and more examples throughout her life of when she had, indeed, been fearless. Had we stopped at this beginning stage, she would have already experienced quite a healing because she was amazed to see all the times she had been fearless.

But we kept talking. I asked the Demartini Method® questions and she answered, finding numerous explicit examples in her life for each question. By the end, she was deeply moved to see that, in actuality, she was equally fearless as fearful. She acknowledged both traits in herself – and here's the kicker, she also recognized both traits in the other person whom she had seen as only fearless. Furthermore, she saw her traits equal to the other person's traits in intensity. She saw all in balance.

Then she took action on her "new-found" fearlessness. As her fearless self, she went to meet with the other person and, for the first time, the communication between them was easy. She got the signature on a document that she wanted, and this "much feared event" was actually cordial. Their interaction was a distinct change in behavior for both of them from all their previous encounters.

So in this work, nothing is released, called "bad," or in any way judged. It's all taken into balance and transformed into love.

My first experience going through the process dealt with the underlying causes of my food addiction and weight. One of the key traumas that led to my problem was being sexually abused at age four and never talking about it to anyone for 40 years. One of the main beliefs I took on from that event was *"men are self-serving."* They do what they want for themselves and I end up paying the price. That's an appropriate thought for a little four-year-old who's been abused. But it's not healthy for an adult. Unfortunately, guess what kinds of situations I drew into my life as a result of that belief?

Using Skype for our sessions, Jon Robson guided me through the process to balance that trait I attributed to men. I thought I would be giving him examples of how that pattern repeatedly showed up in my life. Instead, he completely turned the table on me and asked, "So, tell me all the ways that *you* are self-serving."

What!? I was shocked. Wait! We're talking about men here, not about me. Well, apparently we were *not* going to talk about men because I spent the next 40 minutes listing all the explicit times and ways I'd been self-serving throughout my entire life. This process had me take responsibility for having that trait I accused men of. Not only that, Robson then had me list all the *benefits* of my being self-serving, and then all the *downsides* of my not being self-serving. His goal was for me to come to the point where I could *own* both sides of the trait and see that both sides *balanced* each other out perfectly.

The results of this first of many sessions were astounding. By the end of it, I could have gotten down on my knees and kissed the feet of the boy who had abused me. I felt nothing but love and gratitude for him and what had happened. I could see the magnificence of that event because it fundamentally changed my life. I wouldn't have changed any elements of it because all of it helped make me who I am today.

I developed some of my primary skills as a therapist as a result of that incident. It was, and still is, an extraordinary feeling to have complete peace and resolution within me. Previously, I had done a lot of work on this limiting belief, but nothing compared to this work – to bring it to a peaceful close. This was also the session that released my dislike of physical exertion, as well as made a fundamental shift in my food cravings.

After a few months of these sessions, I realized that I wanted to learn how to do this work with my own clients. As much as I have helped clients transform their lives with my hypnosis and belief systems work, I knew this work goes deeper and resolves deep, tough issues in ways I haven't seen before. So I attended the introductory weekend Breakthrough Experience° which is Dr. John Demartini's signature two-day program incorporating the revolutionary new personal and professional development methodologies, The Demartini Method® and the Demartini Value Determination Process™. In The Breakthrough Experience®, Dr. Demartini assists individuals to transform relationship issues, whether personal or professional; empower and inspire all areas of life from finance to family, career to social, mental to physical. He assists in awakening a strong sense of purpose and shows how to overcome challenges in order to catalyze true greatness and potential.

Two months later, I went back for more and attended the five-day training intensive so that I could begin to facilitate this work with others. As I edit this final draft, I am on the plane headed for more training.

I believe that if you want to fundamentally change your limiting beliefs and finally let go of deep wounds that have scarred you for life, Demartini has a process that works. In his many books he includes the actual process for you to go through on your own. If it appeals to you, or you really want to delve deep, his weekend workshop is well worth attending.

SET A CLEAR INTENTION WITH AN ELEVATED EMOTION

Dr. Joe Dispenza is another brilliant facilitator who is dedicated to helping people heal from old wounds and create the life of their dreams. The back cover of his 2014 book *You Are the Placebo: Making Your Mind Matter,* reads

> "Dr. Joe Dispenza, D.C., author of *Breaking the Habit of Being Yourself* and *Evolve Your Brain,* has a passion for teaching others how to use the latest discoveries from neuroscience and quantum physics to reprogram their brains, heal illness, and lead more fulfilled lives. Dr. Joe is one of the experts featured in the film *What the BLEEP Do We Know?* He teaches workshops and lectures all over the world. If you saw the movie years ago, he's the one sitting in front of the fireplace talking about how he begins each day by visioning how his day will proceed, asking for definite signs to further him in his vision. He's also designed a corporate program that brings his model of transformation to businesses."

In his meditations and workshops, he leads you into deep meditation, having you focus on your breath and relaxing your mind and body. He then has you bring to mind a trait or behavior you wish to change, and leads you through the process of releasing it. And then, most importantly, he leads you into the emotional and mental imagery of what you want to create in its place. He says that you need "elevated emotion" so that your body will feel as though the new behavior is already so true that it will create it in physical reality.

This is oversimplified, but basically he teaches you to replace the old behavior with a new vision to create a new reality for yourself. He's very much into scientific research, how the brain works, and how to change beliefs. And like Demartini, Dr. Joe's approach is profoundly life changing for physical conditions, mental thinking, and emotional upsets.

Dr. Joe's passion for his work and helping others to make profound and rapid changes in their thinking comes through loud and clear in his CDs, lectures, meditations, and writings. He is an expert in this field. On page XXXV, he writes:

> "...in order for you to change your beliefs and perceptions, you must combine a clear intention with an elevated emotion that conditions your body to believe that the future potential you selected from the quantum field has already happened. The elevated emotion is vital, because only when your choice carries an amplitude of energy that's greater than the hardwired programs in your brain and the emotional addiction in your body will you be able to change your brain's circuitry and your body's genetic expression, as well as recondition your body to a new mind (erasing any trace of the old neurocircuitry and conditioning)."

150

He clearly and scientifically explains how the brain and body can be changed and rewired to a new way of thinking and being, thereby creating a whole new life experience for you. He teaches repeatable step-by-step instructions for changing your thinking. He notes that by understanding how your mind works, you can learn how to unlearn negative habits and emotions to eliminate self-destructive behaviors, and rewire your brain with new thoughts and beliefs that will help you heal your mind and body and create new results. In the back of his *Placebo* book is a script for an hour-long meditation to help you change your perceptions and beliefs.

On his web site, www.drjoedispenza.com, he offers live monthly tele-classes, Pay-Per-View intensive workshops, books, his events schedule, products, and much more.

During his workshops, he helps people who are in tremendous suffering. One attendee, for example, released chronic debilitating physical conditions from the symptoms of Parkinson's disease. Another – a paraplegic – stood up from his wheelchair after a meditation.

Dr. Joe has found answers on how to move into the quantum field of all possibilities and teaches others how to create the future they desire to become manifest now. It's extraordinary work. He's dedicated to helping the world heal and is definitely living his passion.

WORLDWIDE HELP

These are just two of the great teachers whose work can help you transform your thinking and your life. Their approaches are very different and yet they are united in their desire, focus, and missions to help people fundamentally change the quality of their lives.

The good news is that there are many more teachers all over the world who can help you. In Part IV, I list various resources that use different techniques to help people change their thinking. This is by no means an inclusive list. It's just a beginning point for you to explore.

With the onset of so many online seminars and blogs, all you need is Internet connection to take advantage of a wealth of information. Using Skype, you can now access practitioners all over the world. You are no longer at such a disadvantage because of where you may live. Literally, the world is at your fingertips and there is a plethora of help available to you.

Now let's move from looking backward to moving forward in life.

EMPOWERING THOUGHTS

- You have the innate ability to resolve something within you and to make it happen.

- You can turn the worst thing that has ever happened to you into an event for which you now have immense gratitude.

8

Change Your Future

"*I learned this, at least, by my experiment: that if one advances confidently in the direction of his dreams, and endeavors to live the life which he has imagined, he will meet with a success unexpected in common hours.*" Henry David Thoreau, *Walden: Or, Life in the Woods*

Now that I've spent all this time talking about going into the past and transforming your beliefs so that you can improve your quality of life, let's move into how to transform your life by looking toward the future. I firmly believe that we all need to address both directions in order to create the life we desire.

On the one hand, if you ignore the subconscious beliefs and only focus on what you want to create, your old limiting patterns can keep you recreating the same outcomes – and you will wonder why your visualizations and affirmations aren't working. On the other hand, if you ignore visioning, planning, and taking action steps to create your future, you may transform your limiting beliefs but you haven't given yourself a goal of where you want to go – so you drift and meander and don't move towards what you want.

If you always do what you've always done, then you'll always get what you've always gotten. If you don't want to repeat old patterns, what do you want instead? Diligently work on both sides of the equation to better ensure that you actually can create the life of your dreams.

CREATE YOUR VISION

In 1959 Earl Nightingale partnered with Lloyd Conant and released the recorded message of *The Strangest Secret*, which says that the strangest secret is "you become what you think about." This is one of the most powerful laws of the Universe, and it's what this book is all about. So now, let's begin using our thoughts for our highest good – rather than using them against ourselves to hold us back from the abundant, high-quality life we desire and deserve.

One of the first bestsellers in this area was by Napoleon Hill, *Think and Grow Rich*, which teaches how to use our mind to create what we want. Since then, countless books and teachers have brought forth this wisdom. It's powerful work, especially when combined with releasing whatever keeps pulling you into past thinking.

The main premise and teaching is this: We each have the power within us to choose our thoughts, and by deliberately choosing what we think about, we create our life experience. It takes more than thinking about it once or twice, though. We must make a daily practice of directing our thoughts and emotions towards a specific goal or intended target. We need to put ourselves into our future vision, and actually feel the emotions of how we will feel when we are in that future self we are designing in our mind.

In doing this work, we essentially override and rewrite our old limiting beliefs. Some of these beliefs have had a stranglehold on us – and yet, they *can* be transformed. You can move out of the lifestyle you have been creating through those limiting beliefs and into the lifestyle that you consciously create.

As you now know, your outdated beliefs were created in energy and emotion, and have become habitual, automatic responses. To override them takes concerted effort and discipline, and stronger and clearer intention and emotion. In overcoming your habitual way of thinking you shift from having your unconscious thoughts in charge to putting your conscious intentions, visions, dreams, aspirations, and goals in charge.

All the leading speakers, authors, and thinkers in this field of creating from our thoughts have a similar message: There is a scientific, repeatable way of thinking that produces desired results. These leading proponents have different slants on the "how to," but they all usually come down to a few basics:

1. First, create a clear vision in your mind of the outcome you desire. Then write it down *as though it has already happened*, or draw it in pictures, or create a vision board with pictures and descriptive words of your desired outcome.

2. Second, read your vision daily, imagine and feel yourself already having that life. Look at your vision board and experience yourself living that outcome. Put yourself into the future and act as though it's now. Step into that "future you" and feel what it's like. It takes active, strong

feelings to impress this new way of being upon your subconscious.

3. Third, take action steps toward your desired future life. You can't just dream about it. Every day, do something that moves you toward that life. Plan your day so that you include something tangible that you'll do, even if it's a small move in the direction of your dream. "Act as if" you already are that future person. But take care, that doesn't mean you spend money you don't have, acting as if you already have it. Rather, go into the stores and imagine, feel as though, you could buy whatever you want ... without actually purchasing it. Or if you dream of writing a book, create a cover on your computer, print it out and put it around an existing book, making it feel more real to be holding *your* future book in your hands. (I did this.)

4. Fourth, expect success. Maintain the mindset that you expect your vision and actions to become manifest. But stay on guard. If inwardly you think, "This has never worked in the past so it probably won't this time, but what the heck, I'll try," know that you are setting yourself up for failure. It takes a shift in your thinking for you to believe you *can* have it, you are *worthy* of it, and you *deserve* to have it.

Creating the future you desire takes stepping outside your current life and becoming how you want to be. You mustn't be limited to how you live now. Feel yourself stepping into what your heart would love. Call it fantasy or daydreaming, but you can turn it into reality by taking action steps toward that life. It's only a fantasy if you never do anything about it. Once you attain it, it's no longer a fantasy. It's reality.

I like this description of the creative process that I've learned from my coaching: There is an invisible field of substance upon which we impress our thoughts, which then become form and are made manifest.

This is a creative *process*, so you don't just do it once and put it away. Yes, I've heard and read of people who have done vision boards, put them in the closet, and then a few years later they look at the board and realize they've achieved it all. I'm pretty certain that, in the meantime, they were visioning and goal setting, as well as taking action steps. If they pictured a new house or car, it didn't just suddenly appear in their driveway or they didn't find themselves mysteriously holding the key to a new house. They did things in those ensuing years to move towards those goals, even if they had forgotten about the vision board.

Think of all the planning that goes into a wedding. It typically requires a year of thinking, planning, negotiating, talking about it, selecting a site, testing out recipes, trying on wedding gowns, choosing flowers, designing take-away gifts, having bridal showers, and so on and so on. Thousands of hours of planning and dreaming go into this one-day, one-time event.

Imagine what your life would be like if you spent that same amount of time, energy, focus, will power, longing, emotion, and intense concentration on planning your entire life! The results would be stupendous. You would be unstoppable in creating whatever you want. It's not that you would necessarily acquire a lot of material goods, but rather you would become that future person who is confident in your ability to create and manifest. You would be that different person, regardless of the stuff you accumulate along the way. It's not really about stuff, anyway, is it? It's about who you want to *be*: happy, confident, fulfilled, of service, grateful, and so much more.

As you read this, you may be thinking, "I already know that." Perhaps you know *about* this process, but if you're not living it, then you don't really *know* it. To *know* it is to live it and use it daily. To know *about* this process of creating with your thoughts is a big step in the right direction. You now have the recipe for "baking your life." But the recipe is just information, and unless you use this information, it's essentially worthless and lifeless. It is time to start "baking."

"WHAT DO I LOVE?"

"What do I love?" is one of the most powerful questions you can ask yourself. Make it your north star, your guiding light. If you constantly and consistently ask yourself this question, remaining silent with it, going into your heart to hear the answers, you will know the direction to head and what to do next. In the coaching program where I am the student, we always come back to *"What do I love?"* and *"What would I love?"* In fact, we go further. We ask, *"Do I really love each part of my dream?*

When I talk with my clients about this, so often they respond, "I don't know what I love." It's a source of anxiety and disappointment for them. They honestly think they don't know what they love. So I set them on the process of discovering it: Spend time each day writing down what you notice that you love, or even just like or appreciate. It could be:

- Seeing the morning dew puddle on leaves,

- Lounging in the soft, warm sun,

- Hearing a child laugh with delight,

- Doing a jigsaw puzzle,

- Enjoying a delicious lunch,

- Helping a co-worker solve a problem,

- Riding a motorcycle,

- Reading a book,

- "Shooting the bull" with friends,

- Receiving a special look from a loved one, or

- Having your dog or cat rub up against your leg.

Start small because you are going to improve upon this practice. There is always something in a day that you can love or like or appreciate, even if you are deeply depressed. Find that something and notice that you enjoy it.

If this is difficult, then know this: You have a *belief* that you don't know what you love, or would love to create in your life. That's a false belief because we all are hardwired with knowing how to discern what's in our heart. But if it's not a habit you've cultivated, you need to begin again to learn how to discover what you love.

Don't start with the big overarching question of what would you love to do for a living, what would make your heart sing, or what your purpose in life is. Begin with all the small things you love and appreciate each day.

Write down what you notice that you love. You can start by specifically looking at nature, where there is always beauty and majesty. Is there a specific flower or color or plant shape that appeals to you? Write down how it makes you feel. Notice what you're noticing and write it down so that you can come back to it later. You are forming a new habit. It's actually a wonderful habit. It's called: *"What do I love?"*

What makes this habit so wonderful to cultivate is that it leads you straight into gratitude. How can you not be grateful when your heart is filled with love in small moments in your life? Love and gratitude go hand-in-hand. Build your love and gratitude "muscles."

This practice has real health benefits as well. There is nothing so powerful or healing as the energy of love and gratitude. It sends good endorphins through your body, improving your immune system, and bathing your cells in a healthy inner environment.

If you do this practice daily, you're going to become aware that more of your day is filled with noticing what you love, and your feeling of gratitude will continue to expand. You effortlessly move beyond your former small everyday loves into the bigger questions that you long to answer within yourself, such as "for what purpose was I born?" and "what would I love to create?"

Last year when I began being coached by Felicia Searcy, my goal was to finish writing this book. I had begun it a year earlier, but I had gotten stopped in my tracks. My problem, I discovered, was that I didn't love writing. I loved the idea of the book being already finished, but getting there was another story. For me, writing was hard work, and it didn't flow easily. Each week I was faced with "I don't love writing."

I write easily when I'm in the flow, but I couldn't get into the flow, and, at that time, my writing certainly wasn't based in love. So Felicia encouraged me to investigate other ways to get my information out into the world. I bought voice recognition software to see if speaking rather than typing would help. It didn't. We talked about using a ghostwriter, but that didn't resonate with me. I didn't want an intermediary. We even talked about why it was so important that it be written rather than spoken on a CD. I only knew this: This book was within me and it had to come out in written form. Four months went by in this search.

It was in working with the Demartini processes that I finally released my resistance to writing and the fears that blocked me. Then I began to love to write. Along with that, all the work I was doing in the coaching program helped me to be disciplined, set goals, and take the right actions of writing consistently and nearly daily. The weekly coaching continues to be invaluable in keeping me on track with accomplishing my vision and enjoying the journey along the way.

When I have setbacks and don't write for a week or two, I've learned to be with that part of the process as well. I just come back to *"What do I love?"* I would forget: "Why am I writing this book?" "How can I use my book to serve others?" Remembering the answers to these questions would bring me back into the flow of writing again, because in truth, I love to be of service to others. I love to be part of the healing process and watch lives transform.

This is the creation process. We set our sights on what we love, what we desire, and begin to move in that direction by taking action, doing what we need to do. If we get stopped in our tracks, we notice what's in the way. Perhaps it's an old habitual pattern reappearing. If so, recognize it and do what we need to do in order to keep going. Sometimes just recognizing the pattern is enough for us to choose another behavior and keep moving towards our goal. If needed, we work on that pattern to release, transform, or balance it out. Don't get sidetracked, however, into taking all of your attention and energy off your goals and searching back through your past. Most important: keep moving forward.

The path to our dreams is not a straight highway. It's a process of learning and growing along the way, so the path can meander down some unexpected roads. Notice the beauty of those unexpected thoughts and ideas, but make sure you're still headed in the direction of your dreams. Notice if inner resistance has sidetracked you, or if you are off on exciting new roads that add to the value and quality of what you are creating.

COMMITMENT

The following quote is often attributed to Goethe, but it was actually written by Scottish adventurer William Hutchinson Murray in his 1951 book entitled, *The Scottish Himalayan Expedition.*

> *"Until one is committed, there is hesitancy, the chance to draw back. Concerning all acts of initiative (and creation), there is one elementary truth, the ignorance of which kills countless ideas and splendid plans: that the moment one definitely commits oneself, then Providence moves too. All sorts of things occur to help one that would never otherwise have occurred. A whole stream of events issue from the decision, raising in one's favor all manner of unforeseen incidents and meetings and material assistance, which no man could have dreamed would have come his way. Whatever you can do, or dream you can do, begin it. Boldness has genius, power, and magic in it. Begin it now."*

I love this quote. I had it on my refrigerator for years as a reminder that, indeed, I did not know what would occur, or what support would come my way as a result of my committing to a goal.

Your commitment to a desired goal is a powerful force in creation. Commitment means you have made the decision "Yes" to something you want. It can take years, even decades, for some goals to become physical reality. Some goals just take a long time. Or it may be taking so long because you're not fully committed to the outcome. It could be a "nice to have," but you're not doing the inner and outer work to make it a reality. If you just wish something would happen, most often that's not a strong enough intention to bring it about quickly. *Wishing* is not the same as *committing*.

If you really want something, throw yourself into it. Work on your past: Do the inner work of clearing out old patterns and beliefs that keep you from having it. Do an "archeological dig" on yourself to root out the childhood thoughts that feel so natural and comfortable, but don't bring you what you want in life.

At the same time, work on your future: Get very clear on what you want, write down your goals, make it come alive on paper. Draw a picture of it. Put in all the details you want, but leave out *how* you're going to get there. Leave the *how* to Divine action, as William Murray's quote above reminds us. Describe your future life, and how you feel being that person and having that desired life.

Then make sure you love your dream. Is this dream worthy of you? Do you absolutely drool over the thought of having it? Are any aspects of your dream less appealing than other aspects? If so, swap out those little-loved parts. Keep your dream in mind and refine it over time. As you grow, your dream will grow and change with you. So reread it often, imagine it, visualize it, vividly live it in your mind as if you already have it.

And don't miss the part of creation that states: Take Action Steps Daily. Without action steps, your vision is just a fantasy. You make it real by doing what you need to do.

This commitment to your dream will open up new thoughts and ideas. As Murray's quote states, *"All sorts of things occur to help one that would never otherwise have occurred."* That's very true. When you put your attention onto a goal, new ideas come to mind, you meet people who offer you help along the way, or a magazine article or book with exactly the right information comes to you. You become a magnet, drawing to you all manner of support and resources that move you closer to your dream. Synchronicities can become daily occurrences.

This is the reason you don't define "how" your dream will come about. You don't know how it will occur. Yes, you can take action steps and plan your days with specific outcomes in mind, but you don't know the bigger picture of what will spontaneously come into your life to move you along. That's why you can't get bogged down in the "how" it will occur.

Your job is to stay focused on *"What do I love?"* and your commitment will lead you step-by-step. Your part is to take action on the ideas you receive. Some will work and some may not. Anything that doesn't work is not failure. It is just feedback for you to go in another direction. As long as you are clear on your dream, hold the possibility in your mind that all of what's occurring in your life is leading you in that direction.

UNDERSTAND THE RHYTHM OF CHANGE

Once we take a big step, we don't stop. We then can move into the next phase of learning, which could be titled: "I've taken this big step, now what do I do with it?" You step into a higher conscious-ness and enter a new phase of learning and growing. New fears WILL emerge and you may doubt your decision because the going has become more difficult than you expected, or things aren't happening the way you had hoped. We sometimes have a fantasy that when we take a big step, then everything else will magically fall into line. That's not the way it works, for the most part.

Life is made up of cycles of expansion and contraction. It's a natu-ral rhythm in life, in nature, and in our own experiences. As you move through challenges and into a greater sense of yourself, you might expect life to become easier. Instead, more growth and challenges pop up. You may feel you as though you are shrinking back some, constricting, becoming fearful of the next mountain to cross. These feelings and reactions are natural, so expect them. But don't become disheartened. These new challenges indicate that you're making progress. That's how life works.

Your new life can, of course, unfold extremely well. But it doesn't necessarily always turn out the way you expected. You can be on the right path and still face a higher level of decisions and a bigger way of showing up in life. You are called upon to trust yourself and take actions in ways you never had before. New fears show up every time you are at the edge of your experience. That's just how it works. As you reach for higher and higher levels of being all that you can be, new levels of fear will show up with the changes.

But – and this is important – you now have a foundation and a track record of how to successfully move through fears and the knowledge that you can, indeed, surmount fears. So they no longer have to stop you as they did in the past. You can acknowledge them and know that the answers and solutions are within you – and then carry on.

One of the exercises that can help when you're caught in a battle between fear and faith/trust is to give them each a voice. You can journal the dialogue between them. Write down "Fear:" and then let that fearful voice inside you have its say. Write it all down. And then write down "Faith/Trust:" and let the voice of faith or trust and knowing have its say. Write it all down. And then let Fear respond; then let Faith respond. It can go very quickly, especially if both sides are yelling at each other. Get it out of your head and onto the paper. This exercise can be highly therapeutic and enlightening because you get to see what you're really afraid of and how much or how little faith and trust you have in yourself.

WATCH FOR GUIDEPOSTS

Here's how life lessons show up: We're called to do something that scares us. We may feel unprepared, but then, we may realize that, actually, we've already gotten our training wheels. We may have already done smaller versions in preparation.

You have a great idea, you start on it, it's going well, and then you hit roadblocks. Something doesn't feel right, so you get afraid. Then you may think, "This isn't what I really want to do after all, it's not feeling right."

This "interruption" is part of the process – part of the pathway. Our challenge is to discover how to keep going on this creation pathway after the excitement of the new idea has worn off and we're into the real work of changing. Think of something you feel guided to create, perhaps starting a business. Sounds like such a great idea, you've thought about it for years, you've been getting messages saying, "It's time to do it," and it feels right to you. What arises within you, however, may very well be fear, doubt, and insecurity. "I don't know enough. I'm not smart enough. I can't do this. I don't have the money."

All the while, you're asking yourself, "What am I here to do?"

Fear, doubt, and insecurity are actually guideposts on your change pathway. They signal the "change work" you are meant to move through. By starting the business, you learn more about yourself, you grow, and you become more confident. In actuality, creating the finished product of your business may *not* be the most important achievement on a Soul level. Rather, you may be meant to learn the *process* of moving through your fears and turning a vision into physical reality. That may really be what it's all about.

What if *everything* in your life is about the process of doing and becoming, rather than the outcome? I believe the lessons we learn on our pathway are more important than the outcomes. Yes, outcomes are absolutely important on the human, physical level, but the process of growth is what's important on the Soul level. You won't take any of your outcomes with you when you die. Your book, your business, your creations don't make it to heaven. But your growth through obstacles and your willingness to step out of your comfort zone, to provide service and caring for others, those are the aspects of your growth that you will take with you on your Soul's journey.

> *"If you bring forth what is within you, what you bring forth will save you. If you do not bring forth what is within you, what you do not bring forth will destroy you."* Gospel of St. Thomas

EMPOWERING THOUGHTS

- If you always do what you've always done, then you'll always get what you've always gotten.

- Perhaps you know *about* this process, but if you're not living it, then you don't really *know* it.

- We all are hardwired with knowing how to discern what's in our heart.

- *Wishing* is not the same as *committing*.

- These new challenges indicate that you're making progress.

- Fear, doubt, and insecurity are actually guideposts on your change pathway.

PART III

A Soul's Perspective

9

Your Soul's Perspective

Before coming into this lifetime, you – as your Soul/Higher Self – planned what you wanted to learn, experience, and accomplish during your time on earth. Your Soul is calling you to remember your plans.

My work has convinced me that our life experiences, especially our childhood experiences, are a set-up for what we have come to earth to learn and experience. As an immortal soul, we agreed to what we would come to learn. We wanted to grow and develop through life challenges, obstacles, joys, and successes. Our purpose and lessons are part of us, a driving force within, which our soul calls us to remember.

This point-of-view of choosing your life ahead-of-time can be a difficult pill to swallow, especially if your life has consisted of:

- Extreme challenges, or

- Your child suffers from severe emotional, mental, or physical problems, or

- You have lived in a highly dysfunctional and abusive family environment that has caused you untold anguish and misery over your lifetime, or

- You have experienced the horrors of war, terrorism or torture.

"Why would anyone knowingly choose such pain and lifelong suffering?" you ask. "The very concept of choosing such a life with all its downsides can make a person extremely angry and bitter. No one in their right mind would choose this."

And yet...

You are more than your physical body. You are an eternal soul, part of which is contained within your body, which you can refer to as your spirit. But the "bigger part" of your soul is not contained within your physical body. People refer to this bigger part of you as your Higher Self, Soul, or some other word. When you die, your physical body ceases to live but your spirit actually becomes more enlivened as it reunites with your soul. In truth, your spirit inside of you and your Soul/Higher Self are always connected, even when you are not aware of, or able to feel the presence of your Higher Self. This connection becomes very clear the moment you pass out of your body. There are countless books of amazing near-death experiences that illustrate others' experiences of returning home to Spirit.

As an eternal soul, you have incarnated into this physical body to learn lessons and grow *on a spiritual level*. At the very core of each of us, we are expressions or aspects of God/ Source/ All That Is.

While we are part of Source, we are not all of Source. Our goal is to grow towards the Light, towards being a fuller expression of Source. We want to Be and exude those qualities that are a higher expression of Source, such as compassion, love, patience, trust, kindness, creativity, and acceptance.

So we come here to earth because we can't fully learn these qualities in the afterlife. There's nothing against us in the spirit world; there's nothing in opposition to us. As a soul, you do not rub up against anything that would challenge your patience or your love or your compassion, because love is the natural state in the spirit world. We come to earth because there's plenty to rub up against: emotions, physical conditions, our bodies, our economies, relationships, failures, to name just a few. Our ability to move beyond our challenges and into creation is what enables us to grow – and it's why we incarnate. We want to have experiences here that we can't have in the afterlife.

In addition, we are equally challenged to learn and grow by following our heart, our joy, and our passion. Just as we learn and grow by balancing our resentments and limited thinking with all the goodness and joyousness in our life, we can also grow by moving toward what makes us feel alive, rather than what deadens us. Growth is our goal and we each get to choose where we put our focus.

One of the greatest scientific discoveries in recent times is that our universe is growing. It had always been thought that there was only one universe, ours, and that it was finite. Now it's known that there are countless universes "out there," and we are just one teeny tiny little piece of the extraordinary puzzle of "all that is." Even more amazing: The universe is expanding. Second-by-second, it is growing larger, pushing outward. We are part of this same inherent nature to grow and expand, to push our boundaries outward into, as yet, undiscovered territories. Growing in consciousness is part of what we are doing here in human bodies on planet earth as we encounter challenges and opportunities.

You may be gifted with musical talent, so you read all about how to play the piano. You can memorize the notes, keys, and pedals, but until you actually sit down at the keyboard, you aren't playing the piano. Playing the piano, making beautiful music, is the goal. Studying to play the piano is the process to attain this goal, but the studying is not the goal itself.

So it is for us in the spirit world. As soul, we study all about the piano, i.e., we learn all about love, compassion, caring, patience, creativity. But until we come to earth, we don't actually "play the piano." In the spirit world, we can only "study" living in and through love, like reading a book about love. We must come to earth to learn and grow in love and move through our fears. That's truly "playing the piano."

If struggling with "being all I can be" is a major theme in your life right now, you might be thinking, "If only I could get beyond all this low self-esteem, then I can figure out what I'm here to learn this lifetime." Believe it or not, this *is* what you're here to learn: How to get beyond feeling you are less than whole and worthy. Simple, but shocking, isn't it? If this resonates deeply with you, then you probably want to choose another lesson to learn, an easier one, don't you? If this isn't your life lesson, then you may think, "What's the big deal?"

You look at the major life issues and patterns that keep repeating throughout your life, the ones you would pay any amount of money to get rid of. I have, indeed, offered to pay Spirit to get rid of some of my stuff! But it hasn't worked; there's no one "up there" collecting. So, yes, our life can be that frustrating. You may be thinking, "I have done everything and that issue of worthlessness is still here! It's been 30 years and I can't get rid of it. If only I could get that obstacle out of my way, then I could move on with my life and be all I've come here to be!"

Believe it or not, experiences of not being worthy are not obstacles. They are doorways. That's probably the best/worst news I can deliver to you. These "obstacles" are supposed to turn into doorways as you grow through them. They are the learning, the pathway to what you have come to learn. They are turning you into the adult you have come to be. You learn to grow by dealing with them – healing and expanding who you are. You are meant to learn that the limiting beliefs you took on during your childhood are not true. Those early experiences set up the negative limiting beliefs that plague you during your life. They are part of your life's calling. At any moment in time, you can dissolve the illusion of these long-lived limiting beliefs and be free of their impact on your life. You can absolutely know that you are worthy of love and everything else you desire.

Don't we all wish some aspects of our childhood had been different? *If only!*

- If only my father had not been alcoholic.

- If only my mother had been emotionally present for me.

- If only I had felt I belonged and fit in.

- If only we hadn't moved just when I found a best friend.

- If only I had not been abused, or bullied, or ridiculed.

- If only I had been smarter or prettier or popular.

The list goes on, but it all ends in the same place: If only *that* hadn't happened, then my life would have been different, and now I would be happier and more successful.

You may be tempted to think, "If only I'd had a better childhood without that family, I'd be able to be all that I can be." That's partly true, but not the whole truth. Yes, the limiting beliefs you took on during childhood hold you back. Yes, they limit you, but only on the human side. As a soul, they are your ticket to spiritual growth and development. You made a plan before coming into this body: move through those limitations and grow more into your spiritual nature.

Rather than looking at our deep childhood wounds and viewing the resulting limiting beliefs as *obstacles* to our growth and development, I have come to learn that these beliefs are actually our *stepping-stones* to our soul's fulfillment.

If there are a couple of issues that you have done tremendous work on through counseling, energy work, belief systems, affirmations, and behavior modification, and they still continue to haunt and discourage you, take heart. Rather than seeing all your work as failure, you may want to shift your view and think of your issues from your soul's perspective: These are *the* issues that, on a soul level, you *really* want to learn. You have decided that, in this lifetime, you are finally going to conquer these issues – no matter how long it takes.

Here's another example. What if you wanted to learn tenacity and perseverance this lifetime? In this case, it's not the specific issues that are most important to you. It's your tenacity, your ability to keep going toward your end goal. That is your life lesson.

Wouldn't that be something to realize that your life is not about a specific issue at all? For you, it's about perseverance, to keep getting up one more time than you fall down.

To take your soul's perspective, look at the one or two key issues in your life that keep happening, even though you've been working to resolve them. These are the beliefs that keep you attracting the same kinds of situations, the same kinds of people, or the same kinds of challenges. We all have aspects about ourselves that we'd love to change. But it's likely you have a couple of main issues that have been with you since childhood. These are the ones you have come to learn through.

Rather than push them away, look at those issues and say, "I get it. This is what I have come to learn and grow through." If you want to really learn a soul quality, you *must*, at some point in time, experience both its positive and the negative aspects. If you're experiencing the negative aspects of a quality, such as lack of patience, take heart. You're on the path to learning that will eventually move you into the positive aspect of being patient.

I invite you to begin the practice of seeing your greatest obstacles and limiting beliefs as your greatest soul blessings. It may not be easy, but this practice can guide you on your path of living your soul's calling.

WHAT DOES A LIFE LESSON LOOK LIKE?

Do you believe you have come into this life to make a difference in the world? How does your heart answer when you ask yourself this question?

No matter who you are, what education you have, or what you think about yourself, know this to be true: Yes, YOU have come into this world to make a difference. You matter – in a very real way – to all the people you interact with throughout your life. You make a difference in their life simply by being part of it. Your presence, your actions, and your energy all contribute to the lessons they are learning. And, of course, the reverse is just as true. Everyone you meet makes a difference in your life, to some extent.

I'm not saying that you are here to become known on a world-wide basis. That's often the ideal we have – to be known around the world. Yes, there are some who achieve this position in life; that's their reality. It actually is what they have come in to accomplish. For the vast majority of us, however, the difference we make in the world occurs on a smaller scale. Yet, it is no less important on the soul level. No less important.

When you think of having a life purpose, do you imagine it being grandiose, something big and important? Many people do. They are looking for a life purpose or lesson that is impressive or grand:

- A masterpiece they create that lives on as their legacy;

- A way of helping mankind on a global scale;

- A way of making a difference in the lives of millions of people.

They don't want to think it can be as simple as "do what you love." No, not that. Many of us think, "Make it a magnificent purpose!"

Here's a secret that many wise people throughout the ages have found to be true: Follow your heart. That's the right thing to do. Just do what you love. Let your heart-mind lead you to what you have come into this life to create.

I've had numerous clients receive this wisdom from their Higher Selves or Elders during journeys into the consciousness of the afterlife, and they are often disappointed. This simple, yet profound, suggestion seems so mundane. They want something more important to the world. And yet, there is great Truth in this approach to life. You can save yourself a lot of mental gymnastics, anguish, and self-doubt if you look at the obvious: What makes your heart sing when you think about doing it? You can do it for a living, or as a hobby, or just spend time in this fun-filled activity. What brings you joy? What makes you feel alive?

Do you already know what you are meant to do this lifetime? If so, are you doing it? If you're not actively pursuing it, why not? I'm sure you have already asked yourself these simple questions countless times. This isn't meant to have you beat yourself up, yet again, for why you're feeling stuck. This is to help you move on.

The desires of your heart point to your life lessons. They are your soul's messages to you, spoken in "soul language" – feelings. If you are clear that you are here to make a difference on a worldwide scale, that's where you put your attention, intention, focus, and energies. If, however, this desire comes from your thinking and your ego, then it behooves you to look into your heart also. What feelings arise in your heart when you visualize yourself living this life on a worldwide scale? Does it leap for joy? Or does it shrink from fear? Is it just a nice thought but doesn't actually resonate deeply with your inner knowing?

A life lesson can be worded very simply, but take a lifetime or more to master. At the end of the day, or one's life, the only thing that really matters is love. So many people who are close to death, or who have had near-death experiences, report that they now understand that life is all about love.

While I believe it is true that we are all here to learn love, there are different facets to learning love. You may be preoccupied with one aspect more than another, such as self-love, loving others, loving the earth, loving animals, love of God/Spirit, or doing what you love.

When your life ends, you'll be faced with questions about how well you lived your life. Did you love yourself? Did you follow your heart and do what you loved? In your relationships, did you deeply love and serve others? These are the questions your soul wants you to answer with a resounding, "Yes!"

SELF-LOVE VS. NARCISSISM VS. SELFISHNESS

As I write this, I realize that people may confuse self-love with narcissism and self-centeredness. The web site http://thenarcis-sisticlife.com states,

> "A significant difference between a narcissist and someone who has self-love is their ability to tell reality from fantasy. Narcissists are often not grounded in reality and they are oblivious to their imperfections or weaknesses. They embellish their strengths and have an inflated sense of worth and self-importance. Their view of themselves is rarely established with real achievements or merit.

> "People with self-love, on the other hand, can distinguish between what they really are and what they fantasize or dream of becoming. They know their limits and their strengths, admit their weaknesses, and have a realistic sense of their achievements. This is in contrast to the narcissist who lives in a world of daydreaming, pretending, and delusions of grandeur."

If you know a narcissist, or perhaps even live with one, you may notice that they are not able to put themselves into your shoes. They do not have the ability to empathize with others, although they think they do. This is what makes it difficult for narcissists to see this quality in themselves. They actually think they are putting someone else first, yet they are actually self oriented. On the other hand, a person with self-love can understand and relate to other people's emotions and feelings.

I have had many clients who also confuse self-love with being self-ish. In their upbringing, they were taught not to be selfish, which meant to not think about what they wanted or needed. This is important: Self-love is not being selfish.

Selfish is defined as: looking after one's own desires; concerned with your own interests, needs, and wishes while ignoring those of others; demonstrating selfishness; showing that personal needs and wishes are thought to be more important than those of other people.

Self-love is not the same as being selfish because there is no disregard for other people, just a kind regard for yourself.

This doesn't mean that you can go out and spend a lot of money you don't have on yourself, all in the name of self-love. That's not self-love; that's self-indulgence. Self-love doesn't harm anyone nor is it against anyone, although others may not agree with you taking care of yourself instead of them.

If you question whether or not your actions come from self-love or self-indulgence, go inside your inner world. Get quiet and allow your inner wisdom to percolate into your consciousness to give you answers. What does this proposed action feel like? Do you feel happy, freer, or peaceful inside? Or do you feel confused, constricted, or unsettled? Your feelings can give you the answer. Going inside and waiting for a feeling answer can take practice, but you are able to do it. We all are. We are all born with this innate ability to access our inner wisdom. It will be a calm, quiet, neutral voice that is based in love. There's no judgment, criticism, condemnation, excitement, or fantasy thinking from your inner wisdom. If you're experiencing that sort of self-talk, then it's your ego, not your heart-mind. At the core of you, there is only Love.

EMPOWERING THOUGHTS

- Our life experiences, especially our childhood experiences, are a set-up for what we have come to earth to learn and experience.

- These "obstacles" are supposed to turn into doorways as you grow through them.

- Begin the practice of seeing your greatest obstacles and limiting beliefs as your greatest soul blessings.

- Just do what you love. Let your heart-mind lead you to what you have come into this life to create.

- Did you love yourself? Did you follow your heart and do what you loved? In your relationships, did you deeply love and serve others?

10

Five Spiritual Attributes

If after reading this far, you feel as though you are unable to discern your life lessons or if you keep second-guessing yourself, there is another avenue you can take. I believe all of us are here to learn to embody the qualities that are commonly seen as "enlightened" or "God-like." Five of these qualities are:

1. Kindness

2. Trust

3. Gratitude

4. Abundance

5. Acceptance

By no means is this list even close to complete, nor is it necessarily the "top 5" qualities of being a fully realized, enlightened, person. This is a starting place, and these qualities – or rather the lack of them in one's life – is often what leads a person into therapy or self-growth. The lack of any of these qualities may show up in your life as a sense that something fundamental is missing. Too often, we experience the opposite qualities, which will also lead a person to seek counseling or to do intensive inner work.

So if you don't know what your life lessons are, then pick one of these five qualities, or some other quality that you admire or desire. Just pick whatever quality resonates most deeply with you. In Buddhism, compassion and wisdom are paramount to attaining enlightenment, so you may wish to work on those. There are many excellent books on the Buddhist approach to compassion and wisdom, so I won't cover those here.

Perhaps you have a role model, someone who exudes one of these qualities and you'd like to be that way as well. Or it could be that you have one of these qualities already and you want to deepen and strengthen that way of being. It really does not matter which one you choose or why you choose it. The point is: choose one (to start with) and stick to it.

Your goal is to embody this quality for the rest of your life. That's right…through the end of this life. You're making a commitment to yourself to make this way of being a priority and incorporate it into all areas of your life, both for yourself and for others.

If you really do this, at the end of this life you'll be a master at it. You will have made a difference in the lives of every person with whom you come in contact. If you embody kindness for 25 years, how can you not influence others? You'll exude the energy of kindness through your very pores, and others will feel it. You'll innately respond to people from all walks of life, in all situations, with kindness. That's not to say you'll be walking on water, because you'll still have your "off" days. That's human, and it's to be expected. Along with your depth of kindness, you'll also be learning the opposite quality, which could show up at times in your life as selfishness, indifference, or even unkindness.

You might notice that I'm not including the quality of love because I believe that all of the qualities are facets of love. In the English language, there is this one word, love, which encompasses everything from loving chocolate, to loving a pet, to loving nature, to loving a person, to loving to read, to loving Source. We definitely need many more words than just one to describe all these activities. We're all here to learn love. The way we express love is broken down into these qualities as well as others.

So let's delve into these five qualities in more detail to see how to learn these life lessons.

KINDNESS

One of my teachers with whom I studied for four years of intensive Integrated Kabbalistic Healing is Jinen Jason Shulman. I'll never forget the first weekend of training in 2002, sitting in a large circle with about 45 other students. We were strangers at that time, embarking together on a journey of deep inner work. In that first class, one of the students was going on and on about his issues, and I was going crazy inside. I was thinking all sorts of unkind thoughts, such as "get it together" or "get over it" or "OMG, what a loser." I don't remember my exact thoughts but I do remember my mindset. I was screaming inside my mind and I couldn't imagine any other way to respond to such a person. My inner response seemed reasonable and appropriate to me.

And then Jason spoke to this person with such kindness and tenderness, with regard for only his wholeness. I realized I was fixated on the brokenness. I was stopped in my mental madness! I had never witnessed anything quite like this, such a depth of kindness and compassion. I had been reacting to the "issues," while Jason was responding to this student's Being. It was a pivotal moment for me. I wanted to be more like that. I wanted to be kinder because I felt so badly about how unkind I had just been in my head. True, nothing was said verbally, but volumes were being said nonverbally and energetically. It just plain didn't feel good to be so mentally unkind.

Later that weekend Jason talked about how he had been working on kindness for 25 years as part of his Buddhist practice. It was a quality he desired to embody. At the end of the weekend, he gave us one main instruction: Be kind to yourself. I wrote that in big print across the top of my notebook so I wouldn't forget.

Being kind to yourself

It has been 12 years since that weekend and I can say for certain that I am kinder to others and to myself than I was back then. I made it a goal to keep kindness uppermost in my mind and behaviors. Am I always kind? Of course not! Do I have my unkind moments? Of course I do! And as I write this, some of them come streaming into my mind, such as writing an unkind "you did this wrong!" email at 3 am, and then sending it. That is, very simply, never a good idea. And yet, within hours, I was writing the apology email because I knew I had been unkind and I didn't want to be that way with a friend. The more you embody kindness, or any quality, the quicker it resurfaces when you have strayed away from your goal, and the sooner you can take authentic action to remedy the outburst.

What does it mean to you to be kind? How do you learn it if that's not second nature to you? You begin by making the intention to be kind to yourself and to others. You then write a vision of the person you want to become, describing in detail how you exhibit the quality of kindness. In addition, make a slogan for yourself, such as "be kind to me" or "be kind to others" or "kindness rules." Place notes all over where you can see them, as a reminder to be kind. You can put it into your smart phone on an alarm, so every so often you are reminded to be kind. To begin with, make it a point to be conscious of your new activity.

It begins with the outer behavior of being kind to others as well as the inner behavior of being kind to yourself. You can act kindly immediately because that's the place you start. It's a new habit, or a new version of an old habit, so you will grow into it. Over time, and with consistent practice and attention, you will begin to embody this quality. It will become more natural to you. There won't be a need for reminder notes all over the place. Make no mistake, I'm not talking about a few months. To embody any such quality of God, or Love, takes years for it to seep into every pore of your being and simply become a part of who you are and how you act.

Being kind to yourself means that you begin to monitor your self-talk. Chances are there is a lot of unkind chatter going on inside your head. Your first step is to notice these unkind thoughts. You might want to write them down as you think of them so that you become more aware of them. You can't change what you don't notice. Then you can rephrase them into kinder thoughts. Instead of "oh, man, there I go again blowing it!" you can begin to gently tell yourself, "I'm doing better than I did before" or "I'm getting the hang of this." Switch your thinking from putting yourself down to encouraging yourself. That's how kindness shows up inside you.

Being kind to others

Being kind to others may mean that you change your language. Rather than being sarcastic or negative, you begin to be silent. If all you can think to say is something unkind, then don't respond at all. You can grow into encouraging language, but you can always start with silence rather than sarcasm.

Also, begin to monitor your thoughts about other people and notice where you gossip or judge in your mind. Write it all down so that you can see what thoughts are filling your mind throughout the day. Then make a conscious choice to begin rephrasing those thoughts about others, just the way you are doing with your unkind thoughts about yourself.

Being kind doesn't mean that you suddenly have to become a "do gooder" and go out of your way to do everything you can for everyone you meet. Rather, begin with a small goal, such as smiling or saying something nice to a cashier, sales clerk, or service person that you meet during the day. Then work your way up to being kind to someone who is being unkind to you. Decide to not react in your old, unkind way. Rather, hold the intention of being kind and see what you are led to say or do. You could very well surprise yourself. I guarantee that kindness can, and will, show up in your life when you make it your intention.

How the Universe works for your good

If you sincerely intend to embody the quality of kindness, or any other divine quality, I want you to understand how life usually works. When you tell the Universe your intention is to be kind, you will notice one or more people will come into your life to test you on your kindness skill level. That means they will push one of your buttons – a button you generally react to in an unkind manner – perhaps even in a *very* unkind manner. In fact, this person, or persons, will likely push a button that brings out the worst in you. Don't get mad. Don't be unkind. Know that this is their job (assigned by the Universe), even though they may not be consciously aware of this assignment.

You will be given opportunity after opportunity to practice your ability to remain kind in a myriad of situations with people who push your hot buttons. When you're in a hurry, you will encounter rude drivers who pull in front of you and then slow down. Or you may be in for something far more complex, perhaps involving financial betrayal or a relative who is on the opposite end of the kindness spectrum from you.

My sister ran into such an "unexpected opportunity" when she stated in church that she wanted to be kinder. Within a couple of months, guess what appeared in her life? Yes, a test, in the form of a tenant from hell. This young lady was rude, non-responsive, loud, annoying to the neighbors, continually being visited by the police for her boisterous behavior in the middle of the night, and on and on. My sister had never faced such an unkind person. But she tried her best to maintain her kind behavior toward this tenant, no matter what her tenant did. My sister learned that whenever she maintained her own kind demeanor, she felt peaceful inside, regardless of outer appearances in the tenant's neighborhood, which was in a turmoil due to the tenant's chaotic behavior. In the end, my sister even thanked the tenant for being in her life (for those few months, at least), because the tenant had forced my sister to grow in kindness.

The Universe can, and will, come up with many situations for you to reach deep within yourself to draw up kindness. The more you are able to be genuinely kind, the less these "tests" will topple your resolve, and the more naturally you will instinctively become kind in the presence of unkind people.

TRUST

Let's say you want to learn the quality of trust. Here's how you begin to discover what your life lesson is. As a soul beginning to learn how to trust and be trustworthy, you may come into a life surrounded by a trusting family and friends. You therefore naturally learn to trust yourself and others. Betrayal doesn't come into your reality. You live through that lifetime experiencing complete trust. (If you don't accept the idea of reincarnation, then substitute the example of each school year rather than each lifetime.)

At the end of that life, you return to the spirit world and proclaim, "I've got it! I've learned trust!" And your spiritual guides and teachers may say to you, "Actually, that life was just to let you know what trust is like. You were able to experience the end result that you are aiming for. Now your real learning begins."

You next come into a life in a highly dysfunctional family, perhaps with alcoholic parents or mental illness. Your parents lie to you, break promises over and over, and disregard your needs. In addition, your siblings and friends, and later in life, your lovers lie to you. Thus, you learn from the time you are a young child that you cannot depend on the people you should be able to trust.

In that lifetime of learning about trust, you learn not to trust others and not to trust yourself. In the afterlife you realize it was all set up for you to learn to change your consciousness so that you would be able to trust yourself and others.

Learn trust from betrayal

After that life, you incarnate into the next lifetime where you may experience betrayal, which is the opposite of trust. In this lifetime, you experience being betrayed by friends, family, employers, co-workers, and lovers.

You see, we choose our families to help us learn our life lessons. If you are learning about betrayal right now, your soul agreement before coming into this life is for others to seemingly betray you.

The purpose of this betrayal is not to hurt you, although it does indeed hurt and cause great pain. The purpose is for you to learn that it's not true! It's for you to learn that you are whole and complete within yourself, and no one can "betray" you, although it can look that way.

When faced with betrayal, you can get so bogged down in your suffering that you forget what you actually came into the body to learn as a soul. It can be a heavy, miserable life. You just keep attracting those who betray you, and you continue to believe the story you tell yourself, "Everyone betrays me."

You can also live at least one lifetime, if not many, experiencing betraying yourself – in order to learn how to trust yourself. Think of all the ways self-betrayal shows up in your life now, even if it's not a major theme. You may promise yourself that you'll exercise more, watch what you eat, spend more time with your family, meditate more, be patient with an exasperating relative, not gossip or get into other people's business telling them what to do, not do any more drugs or drinking, or countless other ways in which you have good intentions but don't always follow through. You keep breaking your word to yourself about what you'll do.

Even more of a self-betrayal might be to go against your own inner knowing, your intuition, and to make excuses to yourself for your behavior, even when deep down you know better. You know you need to leave a job that deadens you, or a relationship that no longer is supportive or growth-oriented, or friends who are negative and bring you down. And yet, you remain because you are afraid. You ignore the whisperings (and feelings) of your inner self to move on. So then the whisperings become louder and louder, and your fear of moving on into the unknown also becomes stronger, and louder, drowning out your inner voice. We all betray our own inner knowing time and again, because we can be slow to learn to listen and follow our knowing.

This is normal human behavior. It's part of the learning we all go through. We're not aiming for perfection, just awareness and movement toward living more in alignment with our soul's whispering – speaking softly through our intuition.

When you again return to the spirit world, you understand clearly how you got bogged down in the appearance of betrayal and mistrust. It appeared those people actually betrayed you, and on a human level they probably did. But on the soul level, their behavior was meant to create the environment for you to learn about trust, for yourself and others.

So if you find betrayal playing a large role in your life, I'm quite sure you are actually trying to learn trust. You can choose to continue putting your energy into betrayal, or you can switch sides and focus on trust now.

An exercise in trusting

One definition of trust is that you rely on somebody or something, including yourself. If you think you can't trust or rely on others, here's an exercise that can change your perspective.

Write down all the people and conditions you rely on daily. To get you going, this list could include such things as: the water runs when you turn on the faucet, lights turn on when you flip the switch, coffee is available at your local coffee shop, your car starts when you turn the key, the stove works when you turn on the burner, other drivers stop at red stoplights, your eyesight is the same as it was yesterday, and your office or workplace co-workers function much the same as the day before.

When you stop to think about it, most of your daily encounters are based on trust. And yet you can think of yourself as a person who has trust issues. You might want to reconsider or reword your belief about yourself to more accurately reflect your life, rather than believing your limiting belief.

If you want to focus on the quality of trust, you can begin by doing the above exercise every evening. At the end of each day, reflect back, and write down 10 to 20 people and situations in which you trusted or relied upon them to play their role – and they did, indeed, come through for you. This will help you to see that you may already trust far more than you realized. You can build upon this realization by moving your innate ability to trust into more difficult situations.

You can then expand this exercise by listing 5 to 10 ways in which you trusted yourself by following your intuition or knowing during the day – and things turned out well or better than you expected. Begin to affirm all the small ways in which you succeeded in trusting yourself and in following through on your intentions for the day.

There's a saying "where attention goes, energy flows." This is important because if you begin to focus on how you do trust yourself, putting your attention there, then you will find that you begin to have more awareness of trusting yourself and following through. Your energy will flow to trusting yourself and you'll find that you do it more. If, however, you focus on, and talk about, times of mistrust and betrayal for yourself and others, that's where your attention will go. And that's what will grow in your life.

Learning to trust your intuition

I used to teach a class on intuition and the students most wanted to learn how to *really* follow their intuition. I would have them start in this simple way: If there are several possibilities of routes driving home from work, ask yourself which one to take each day. Listen for the still small voice inside. Perhaps it shows up as a sense or a hunch. Follow that hunch and go home that route. *Do not*, however, make the mistake of saying there's a reason for going that route, such as, you'll avoid an accident.

Make it more about just learning to trust your inner hunches, so there's no story involved about how it's a better or safer route. If you practice on small levels, then when it comes times to make bigger and more life-changing choices, you'll be aware of how it feels to trust yourself.

As with kindness, be ready for the Universe to give you opportunities to trust yourself. Even if a crisis appears, or especially if a crisis appears, go inside and listen or feel your knowing. Remember that this looks like it's about the crisis, but more importantly, it's about your ability to trust yourself through the experience.

Learning trust, or any other divine quality, is an ongoing process of experiencing and growing. There is no endpoint when you suddenly have completely mastered this quality; although, you can embody it to the point where trust is no longer an issue for you. You are learning to listen to and follow the immortal part of yourself. This is no small task, and there may not be anything more important for you to master.

Albert Einstein said, "The intuitive mind is a sacred gift and the rational mind is a faithful servant. We have created a society that honors the servant and has forgotten the gift."

Learning to trust others

What about trusting others? How does one go about learning that skill? First and foremost, it's good to remember that not everyone can be trusted. Newsflash: some people lie and deceive as a way of being. They are in your life, in one respect, to be your teacher. Just as important as knowing when we can trust someone is knowing when we can't trust them. If you find your life filled with untrustworthy people, then you have some work to do on your limiting beliefs about living in an untrustworthy world – to release the thinking that's creating these situations.

Use a two-pronged approach to learning to trust others. First, do the belief systems work to go back to the root cause of your belief, *"I cannot trust others,"* and begin to release the energy and emotions wrapped up in this belief. Notice if your lack of trust is limited to a certain relationship, such as lover, friend, male, female, boss, or family member. Do the work to bring your perceptions about trust into balance within you, to see for yourself that you actually already trust others.

You might even want to explore the situations where you do not trust yourself, which leads you to mis-trust others as well. As I've noted earlier, it's never about the other person, it's always about yourself.

Also use the visualization techniques to vividly picture yourself with a friend or lover whom you can trust. Notice more and more who specifically, as well as under what circumstances, you are able to trust another person.

I promise you that these techniques work. You can change your thinking and actions to create the trusting relationships you desire.

Learning to trust the Universe

What do you believe and experience regarding trusting God, the Universe? I have seen in my own work, as well as in what I have read, that we all fall into one of two camps: Either we see the world as a safe place or as an unsafe place. Your perceptions of your childhood experiences set you on one of these two roads. Or, if tragedies or traumas occurred later in your life, you may have lost faith in the world, in God, and decided that you can't trust anything outside of yourself. The brutalities of the world happening in your life can also cause you to absolutely believe that there is no safe place to be, and you can't trust or have faith in anything outside of what you try to control.

No matter what has happened to you, you can learn, or relearn, to trust the Universe. This doesn't mean that whatever outcome or desire you want or pray for, you will receive. That's not how trust works. It's not based on "you give me what I want and I'll trust you." Rather, learning trust is an inner journey, where you connect with your soul, with your immortal self. I'm not talking about believing in a religion or dogma. Rather, you can experience going inside and meeting that aspect of yourself that is not limited to your physical body. This experience is available to every single human being on planet earth. It's hard wired into us. Whether or not you are aware of your soul, it is part of you, it's greater than you, and you can access it.

When you put your attention and intention on learning to trust God, the Universe, All That Is, be ready for some extraordinary experiences. These prayers are answered: "God, I want to know you." "God, let me know you are real and that I can trust you."

Begin with asking for what you want. And then listen for the answers, the guidance, and the path to follow. Your search can lead you on a lifetime of learning and growing, but what else is more important?

Evolving in consciousness

At different points in your life, you are called upon to evolve in consciousness and acknowledge that you know some things to be true. Learn to let your inner wisdom point the way and help you realize that your intuition can be depended on as much as, or even more than, your logical, rational thinking.

I've heard that "faith is fidelity to the insights you've gained." When you have an insight, your doubting mind may step in, making you question or think you are just making things up. My suggestion is to be aware of your doubt. See if it's a familiar, habitual track that you go down. If so, be aware that doubt is not from your adult mind being rational. Rather, it's your childhood doubt (age 4, I don't know, I'm not sure, etc.) rearing up and causing you to fall back.

Acknowledge the doubt and notice the role it plays in your life. How much does it interfere with your instincts or keep you from trusting them? Acknowledge your doubt as one part of your experience, and, at the same time, also validate any awareness or insight you have. Let both your doubt and your awareness exist. Hold these opposites without either one having to take over. Let yourself have doubt, if that's what you need to do, because that helps you break the spell of "I've always thought this way." Also, let yourself have insights and inner knowing that come from a deeper place within you.

As you move along your path, it might be a good idea to have a new mantra. Rather than trusting your doubt, and doubting your knowing, as you have been taught to do, you could begin to live by these words: *Doubt your doubt… Trust your knowing.*

GRATITUDE

Gratitude may very well be the least complicated path to enlightenment. You simply form the practice of being grateful for everything in your life, at all times. It's simple and it's not complicated. But it most definitely is not easy in all instances.

The benefits of being grateful

Robert A. Emmons, Ph.D., is one of the world's leading scientific experts on gratitude. He is a professor of psychology at the University of California, Davis, the founding editor-in-chief of *The Journal of Positive Psychology,* and author of numerous books on gratitude, including *Thanks! How the New Science of Gratitude Can Make You Happier.* In an online article at www.greatergood. berkeley.edu, Emmons defines gratitude as having two key components.

1. First, it's an affirmation of goodness. We affirm that there are good things in the world, gifts and benefits we've received.

2. Second, we recognize that the sources of this goodness are outside of ourselves.

He writes, "We acknowledge that other people – or even higher powers, if you're of a spiritual mindset – gave us many gifts, big and small, to help us achieve the goodness in our lives."

There has been a growing amount of scientific study on positive psychology, which includes gratitude, since the late1990s. Research has repeatedly shown that cultivating gratitude has many measureable benefits. Emmons explains, "Gratitude journals and other gratitude practices often seem so simple and basic; in our studies, we often have people keep gratitude journals for just three weeks. And yet the results have been overwhelming. We've studied more than one thousand people, from ages eight to 80, and found that people who practice gratitude consistently report a host of benefits:

Physical • Stronger immune systems • Less bothered by aches and pains • Lower blood pressure • Exercise more and take better care of their health • Sleep longer and feel more refreshed upon waking

Psychological • Higher levels of positive emotions • More alert, alive, and awake • More joy and pleasure • More optimism and happiness

Social • More helpful, generous, and compassionate • More forgiving • More outgoing • Feel less lonely and isolated."

He found that the practice of gratitude can increase happiness levels by around 25%. A few hours writing in a gratitude journal over 3 weeks can create an effect that lasts 6 months, if not longer.

The magic of writing a gratitude journal

I have always read and heard that a gratitude journal should be written in nightly. Each night you list five things for which you are grateful. It's a routine, a ritual, which many people follow and from which they gain immeasurable benefits. And yet the research now shows that it's actually more effective to write down five things for which you are grateful just once a week. You review your week in your mind and that's when you write your list.

The reason for recommending this weekly practice, rather than the daily practice, is that our minds get bored easily. So a daily writing practice can quickly become routine and we are more likely to get numb to the actual experience of being grateful. It can become more about thinking than feeling. With a weekly practice, however, the surprise element (as opposed to the daily routine) has been shown to instill greater feelings of gratitude.

One of the main elements as you write in your gratitude journal is to take the time to be especially aware of the depth of your gratitude. Relive the experience in your mind and see it as a gift to you. Feel the feelings you associate with being grateful. Savor the good. This is not a "to do" list that you write down quickly and then move on to the next task. Rather, be mindful and present as you express your gratitude in writing.

It's so interesting to me that my own experience matches the research. In my coaching program, I am to write down five things I'm grateful for each morning. Once a week during the coaching call, we start by writing down one thing we're grateful for from the previous week. I have found that I list my morning gratitudes much like a to-do list. I don't make it a deep experience for myself. Yet on the weekly call, I go inside myself to really find what I'm grateful for and feel it more deeply. I savor it, as Emmons says. As with anything, notice your own experience and let that be your guide.

While Emmons recommends writing just once, or even twice, a week, he does recommend a daily morning practice of generating a gratitude list in your mind as you wake up. What are you looking forward to that day? What are you grateful for as the day begins? I love waking up and thinking about the day and the people I'll be seeing, or what I'll be doing, and offering thanks for the day to come.

And, of course, there's the practice of being grateful throughout the day. It's such a simple act, "thank you," but it can work miracles in your life and in the lives of others. For an exercise, see if you can say "thank you" 1000 times within a month. You'll find you are more conscious of your gratitude, and that's the whole point.

The many ways to say "thank you"

Another way to cultivate gratitude is to write a letter of thanks to someone important in your life – someone whom you have not properly thanked. Be specific in the letter. Give details of why you are grateful to this individual and how the individual's behavior affected your life. It's most effective if you then deliver this letter in person, or read it to them over the phone, or on FaceTime or Skype, rather than just mailing it to them. Be present to this important person as you thank them for specific ways in which they have enhanced your life.

What if you were to write a letter like this each week for six or eight weeks, or each month for a year? As you write each letter, and deliver it in person to the important people in your life, then you can journal what that experience was like for you. At the end of the year, or whatever length of time you choose, you would have a rich testimony to the depth and power of gratitude. I promise you, it will change your life.

Another way to practice the quality of gratitude is to say "thank you" more often. How easy is this? And yet, when you make it a mindful spiritual practice, it takes on a richer quality. Each day you can look directly into someone's eyes and say, "thank you." Bring your whole self into your gratitude. This means that it's not saying, "oh, thanks" in passing, as we so often do. Rather, this is a skill you develop over time so that you can be very present to another person and fully express your appreciation to them. If you have small children, get down on their level, eye to eye, and tell them "thank you!" for whatever they have done or for just being who they are.

In this day and age of email and Twitter, thank-you notes have become much more informal than in the "old days" when I was growing up. As children, we siblings had to write thank-you notes for every gift we received from our grandparents and other relatives, especially for birthday and Christmas presents. This started as soon as we could print on our own. My grandmother saved all of the letters she received from her six grandchildren, so I'm sure they meant a lot to her. It's a real treasure to have them now. This discipline seems to be slipping away from our society, and yet it's a powerful force of gratitude.

It's different to have a note that is handwritten versus a typed email or tweet in 140 characters or less. Yes, any type of gratitude can be appreciated. However, to cultivate this quality of gratitude, you might want to consider the old-fashioned hand-written notes sent through the postal service. This practice isn't just in response to gifts you've received. What if you began to write your friends or family a short "thank you for ..." and then mention some specific action or quality you noticed in them that week. Or you can send an "I was thinking of you – thank you for being in my life" note. Make it a practice to send one such note every week. It forces you to go into the mindset and feeling of gratitude, and then express it in written form.

Gratitude and happiness

If you do these simple practices on a regular basis, you will cultivate the quality of gratitude so that you can call upon it when needed. If you're having a hard time, or find yourself caught in negativity, remember one of the many instances of gratitude that you've written about and bring back that good feeling. The more you are able to generate the feeling of gratitude at will, the greater your ability to not get swept away by negativity.

Think about this: gratitude can reduce resentment and other negative emotions because you can't focus on both resentment and gratitude at the same time. If you focus on what you're grateful for, then you are not as aware of who or what you resent. The resentment gets pushed further down in your consciousness and gets less of your attention. This is how you feel happier.

When you think about it, it makes a lot of sense that practicing gratitude will increase your happiness. It makes you pay attention to what's going on in your life and to notice when you are grateful. This is the spiritual practice of mindfulness, of being present. Notice what you are noticing. Be aware of what you are experiencing throughout the day as you are on the lookout for what you can be grateful for. Your attention on gratitude can have a snowball effect, as the more you are on the lookout for it, the more you will become aware of all the every-day opportunities you have daily to be grateful.

For myself, it's a daily practice throughout the day to be grateful. While I'm not constantly grateful, by any means, I do notice what I'm grateful for on a continual basis. This ranges from the beauty that surrounds me, to being grateful there's no snow on the ground, to savoring my friendships and clients, for the awareness of being aware, and so much more. There's absolutely no limit to the amount of things I – and you – can find that can fill us with gratitude.

Being grateful during dark times

So now we come to the other side of gratitude: How to be grateful when tragedy strikes, losses occur, or your life hits some very big bumps in the road. This is when the small daily practices of gratitude come into greater importance.

Here's a truth: Life is balanced, even when it doesn't feel that way. There is a Divine Order in all the seeming chaos. We just can't see it sometimes. So know that each bump has a "gratefulness" aspect. Look for it. Know it is there.

Cultivating the practice of gratitude does not mean that you are grateful that something happens, but you can be grateful when, or in spite of, some difficulty in life. After the 9/11 attacks, people became more grateful. They suddenly realized that life is precious and to be appreciated. No one was grateful *that* it happened, but people became more grateful *because* it happened.

If you receive devastating news, such as the death of a loved and cherished person, it may take some time before you can hold the seemingly opposite emotions of sadness at the loss as well as gratitude for the blessings you received from that person. The same can be true with a life-threatening diagnosis. You become acutely aware of your mortality, and can become much more grateful for each day, each person, each experience you have. Disease can sharpen your view on life so that you notice more and are more present to each moment. Gratitude can increase immeasurably under such circumstances, but it can take some time. It's not always immediate. We're not robots who can turn off our feelings and emotions and come into equanimity with the news of loss.

In the darker times of life, it can take time to find anything to be grateful for. In the midst of a crisis, all you might be able to do is to know that someday you will see the blessings. Someday you will find gratitude. That consciousness sets into motion the intention to find gratitude, even when that doesn't seem possible from a logical point of view, such as with a violent death or loss of a young child. When a tragedy seems pointless, there can still be gratitude and blessings that flow from it. It's all in your intention. It's all in your own hands.

Learning to bless everything

Anything and everything that comes into your life is an opportunity for you to grow and develop your consciousness. If you truly believe this, it's easier to move more quickly into gratitude because you know that, no matter what is happening, there is a blessing inherent in the situation. Sometimes you have to look deeply below the human level to find it. But know that there is always a positive intent on the soul level. Part of the journey in raising your consciousness, becoming more aligned to your soul's purpose, and fulfilling your life lessons involves developing a deep inner appreciation and acknowledgment of the divine order taking place in your life.

Gratitude is a choice. It's a quality you can develop and cultivate through simple practices. It will serve you mightily through life's difficult days, as well as enhance your well being and happiness on a daily basis.

ABUNDANCE

The very nature of Source is abundance. There is no lack of any kind within God/All That Is. The only lack is in our minds, in our thinking, and in our actions. Our subconscious beliefs, along with our actions, determine the level of abundance we enjoy or feel deprived of.

If you choose abundance as a quality that you want to embody, do you automatically think that you would concentrate on money and financial prosperity? That's typically what comes to mind first when one thinks of abundance: money, wealth, and possessions.

Yes, wealth is one form of abundance and it's an important one, especially if you are sadly lacking in it. If you are in financial survival, then it's likely you believe that abundance would mean relief from worry and stress about paying bills, making ends meet, and having the ability to provide the lifestyle you desire for your family.

Well, perhaps. But, I need to point out that if you are working with qualities attributed to higher consciousness, then you probably won't be concentrating on money, will you? That doesn't resonate as consistent. Source is already abundant. It does not know lack.

So if abundance is not about money and possessions, then what does it entail? What aspects of this quality would you embody in order to live in abundance?

Ways to view abundance

Abundance is actually not about things; it's all about consciousness. Embodying the quality of abundance in your life means that you are raising your consciousness to a higher level – to the level where you would see abundance in all things, all places, and in all conditions. It's much like gratitude in that it's a mindset that grows over time. As you embody abundant thinking, you begin to see the world through this new perspective, then you act from abundance, and then you experience abundance.

This perspective of abundance embraces lack and limitation as well as surplus and excess. Abundance takes into consideration the entirety of all that is and finds nothing lacking, even when the physical conditions appear to shout out, "THIS IS LACKING!"

In the face of physical conditions that demonstrate "lack and limitation," choose Truth, which is the abundant nature of the Universe. This means that you learn to affirm, look for, and believe in abundance, even when it seems to be missing. You may think that you don't have enough money to pay your rent or other bills at the end of the month. You can look in your checking account and measure it against your bills. They don't match. The bills add up to more than you have in your account.

Embodying abundance

To embody abundance, begin to affirm all that you do have and all that is available to you. Then notice your thinking. What limiting thoughts are screaming in your head as you affirm abundance?

Is your mind screaming something along the lines of, "Are you crazy? There's not enough money no matter how many times you say you're abundant!" Realize that these thoughts, and similar ones, are creating your physical conditions of lack.

Living the quality of abundance requires that you notice such limiting thoughts and challenge them, question them, or balance them out with empowering thoughts. If you are always thinking, "I don't have enough money," then begin to notice all the ways in which you do have enough money – even where you realized you had more than enough money. This shift in thinking is how you begin to affirm the positive, and replace the negative.

To help you begin to change your mindset, you might want to count the number of books you own, or the number of articles of clothing, or the number of utensils in the kitchen, or tools in the garage, or toys your children have. Pick whatever you want, but count how many you have. This act demonstrates your abundance. You have enough.

In fact, you may have more than enough. Do you have an over-abundance of toys, tools, shoes, or utensils in your home? Abundance is not "surplus and excess." If you have too many of something, ask yourself, "Why?" What's your underlying fear that has to do with not having enough?

Next, move beyond just thinking about abundance in terms of money and begin to affirm all the marvelous ways in which this universe is abundant. You can start by noticing how many new inventions and designs are created each and every year, year after year after year. There is such unlimited creativity and innovation in technology that we can hardly keep up with all the new gadgets and upgrades to our devices. Think of all the creativity that has created all the new gadgets that we didn't even know we needed – and now we think we can't live without them. That thinking comes from a consciousness of abundance. These creators are not limited to what they can create or what people think is possible. They can create seemingly impossible things. Just take a look around you.

The creators of the next generation of "got to have it" gadgets are certainly not thinking in terms of lack or limitation. They have got to have beliefs in line with "anything is possible." This is one aspect of the abundance quality. Anything and everything is possible because God/All That Is includes everything already created as well as all that will ever be created.

Abundance consciousness fosters this same mindset: If you can think it up, it can be done.

That, however, is not the consciousness most of us have. We have our limiting thoughts, which are our barriers to stepping out into true abundance.

Neutralizing limiting thoughts

To embody abundance we need to deal with and neutralize our habitual limiting thoughts, reactions, and emotions. Begin by noticing every single time you pull back, hesitate, or in any way stop the free flow of energy moving through you.

Try this exercise: Set a timer for five minutes and during this time notice all your thoughts – every single one. How many of them are limiting in some form or manner? How many minutes, or seconds, did it take for the first limiting thought to pop into your mind? Perhaps that happened within seconds, with a thought like: "This is stupid," or "I can't do this," or even "Is it time yet?"

This exercise will help you become aware of how much of your consciousness is *not* based in abundance. Then your real life work begins: going deep inside where you (1) do the heavy-duty work of clearing out the underground habitual limiting thinking that rules your life, and (2) begin to bring your thinking into alignment with abundance consciousness, that everything you need is provided and available to you. Look for it and find it.

As I write this, I want to remind you that your path to embodying the quality of abundance may be very different from anything I have written. That's great! It just goes to prove that this is an abundant universe and I am only offering a few suggestions. You can follow your own path. There is so much more than anything I have written, or could ever write about abundance and all the other God qualities. I'm here to help you open the doors to your heart and soul, but by no means do I have your answers. This is an abundant universe and that means you have unlimited ways to fulfill your life lessons and purpose. Sometimes we just need a few ideas to get us going. That's what I'm doing in this book and in my work: helping you to get into the flow of your own life.

ACCEPTANCE

Did you ever play with the childhood "finger trap" in which you put your right pointer finger into one end of the woven toy and your left pointer finger into the other end? The more you pull to get them out, the tighter the trap becomes on your fingers. The only way out is to let go, to move your fingers inward, toward each other. When you fight "what is," you get caught in the resistance and struggle, and you can't get loose. When you let go, by moving inward, then the trap releases and your fingers can escape. This simple toy illustrates the quality of acceptance.

Wikipedia.com defines one form of acceptance as: "Acceptance in human psychology is a person's assent to the reality of a situation, recognizing a process or condition (often a negative or uncomfortable situation) without attempting to change it or protest it. The concept is close in meaning to 'acquiescence,' derived from the Latin 'acquiēscere' (to find rest in)."

I have been having a difficult time deciding which fifth quality to write about. I've started three other qualities, and within about two sentences, discarded them. I wondered if writing about only four qualities would be sufficient, although I knew I wanted five. Finally, tonight, I got quiet, went inside myself into prayer, and asked for help. I quit trying to find the "right" or "best" quality. I quit fighting with myself. Within moments I had my answer.

As humans, we are conditioned to resist and to fight against what we don't like. Don't accept that which is unacceptable! It makes sense, doesn't it, to rail against what offends us or in some way is not good enough so that we can change it and make it acceptable? We tie up so much of our mental and emotional energy in fighting against the circumstances that we have judged and determined to be wrong in some way.

There is, however, another way to live life that embodies a higher consciousness and awareness of spiritual laws. I believe acceptance can be a sacred gift that you give to yourself or another. To accept a situation that is not to your liking can be difficult and challenging – but also so very, very liberating.

Learning to accept what is

Why would you want to embody this quality and accept life as it is, especially the unacceptable aspects of it?

This often-quoted paragraph on page 417 on acceptance in *The Big Book of Alcoholics Anonymous* answers that question. You can substitute any situation that applies to you for the word "alcoholism," and this will fit:

> "And acceptance is the answer to *all* my problems today. When I am disturbed, it is because I find some person, place, thing or situation – some fact of my life – unacceptable to me, and I can find no serenity until I accept that person, place, thing, or situation as being exactly the way it is supposed to be at this moment. Nothing, absolutely nothing, happens in God's world by mistake. Until I could accept my alcoholism, I could not stay sober; unless I accept life completely on life's terms, I cannot be happy. I need to concentrate not so much on what needs to be changed in the world as on what needs to be changed in me and in my attitudes."

So many of us formed the childhood belief that if we don't like something, then we need to be unhappy about it or else it won't change. It is inborn in us as infants to cry when we are unhappy because we are hungry, or wet, or sleepy. Something is "off" in our little world and our only means of making it better is to cry. As we grow into childhood, we complain or whine about what we want or don't want, hoping perhaps Mom or Dad will do something to make us happy again. If this behavior works well for us, the pattern becomes more entrenched as it follows us into adulthood where we live in a state of "what's wrong with me, you, and life in general?"

We don't yet have the consciousness to accept it as it is. We still want to take action to change the situation. There is usually fear underneath this non-acceptance – fear that nothing will change and we'll be stuck with what we don't want.

Make no mistake: You can be happy and accept what is in your life, and still want more or better. Both are true at the same time. But accepting "now" is crucial for inner peace of mind.

The truth lies in what seems to make no sense to our logical mind. By accepting life "as is," we can find inner peace and happiness. As long as we're fighting against any aspect of (1) who we are or (2) how others are, we will continue to be in the consciousness of dis-ease, discontentment, and general unhappiness. This is not the path to peace and well being.

Many books have been written on this subject so that you can begin to learn how to embody acceptance. A couple of my favorites are well known: *The Power of Now* and *The New Earth*, both by Eckhart Tolle, and *Loving What Is* by Byron Katie. Byron Katie's work, which she calls The Work, is a simple and brilliant process of four questions that help you to come to accept "what is." You can go online to her web sites, www.byronkatie.com and www.thework.com, where she has many videos of working with clients. So you can learn the process yourself. I've been to several of her workshops and she is amazing in the ways she uses her process to transform lives and release mental suffering. I spent a year doing her work with a group of women, meeting every Friday morning for three hours with a facilitator who walked us through the process. It's well worth checking out if you are caught in the web of your mind, fighting "what is."

As I've described in the other qualities, if you make the commitment to embody this quality, then life will hand you the opposite so that you can master the quality. In this case, unacceptable situations may, or will, begin to show up in your life. If you already have a life full of unacceptable people, places and things, then perhaps you already unconsciously have chosen this path of learning. It's time to make your inner work conscious and committed.

My experience accepting what was

I spent three years learning how to accept the unacceptable. My teaching wasn't dramatic or life threatening, as is the case with those who have lost limbs through a tragedy, or have cancer or other serious diseases they need to come to terms with. Mine was simply accepting incredible embarrassment.

Through a series of events, I moved into a tiny room of less than 300 square feet in the basement of a house. It had a door to the driveway, so I had an outside entrance, and it had a hot plate for cooking, a mini refrigerator, and space for a twin bed and a chair. This is where I lived and worked for nearly three years.

I was terribly embarrassed to have clients come into this space, which was not luxurious by any stretch of the imagination. My ego was crushed as I ranted against the Universe, "I have 19 years of education and this is the best I can create? This is not OK!" Clients would ask, "Where do you live?" and when I answered, "Here," I could see their expressions change. I was mortified to have them there, and yet I needed to earn a living.

It didn't take too long for me to catch on that acceptance was my lesson to learn, but I was a slow learner. Whenever I looked in the newspaper for other places to live, I could literally feel angel wings around me, as I heard, "Don't move!" I was determined to be out of there in three months, although the moment I saw that apartment, I knew it would be three years.

I packed my storage unit as though I would be out in three months, so all my winter clothes were in the back of the unit. I think I moved every box in that unit no less than five times during my three-year stay. I cried, I complained, and I worked on my inner world until I eventually came to peace within myself.

My real acceptance wasn't, "ok, this is fine." Rather, real acceptance came in the form of, "I am grateful for this room, just the way it is. I am happy here. I can stay here and be at peace."

Once I found the peace inside me that I had been searching for, the fight inside me was over. It was then that the owner of the house upstairs moved out and I moved up into the main house.

Today, if I encounter anything that I consider "unacceptable," I would do all the techniques I know, and perhaps move to balance and peace within a few hours or sessions, rather than three years.

Learning self-acceptance

Self-acceptance is a life lesson for many people. Each and every person who fights against their body image, weight, beauty, height, or any other aspect of their physical form, is learning self-acceptance. We have an image of how "perfect" we should be, and when our body does not match that image, then we call it "unacceptable" and fixate on how to make it better.

The multi-billion dollar beauty, diet, and exercise industries are founded on the premise that you can look better than you are. I'm not against makeup and exercise, but it's our inner world that suffers terribly when we are unhappy with our body.

Self-acceptance means that you approve of yourself as you are, right now. You appreciate yourself for all that you are, and you validate yourself for being the person you are. It's this simple: You accept yourself *as* you are, not how you could be or should be. Learning self-acceptance can be an entire life's work.

This doesn't mean, however, that you use this as an excuse for continuing "bad behavior," such as carrying resentments or being sarcastic. "Well, that's just how I am" is not what self-acceptance is about. Rather, this is a spiritual path in which you do your inner work to soften the corners of your abrasive traits and emotional swings, to move closer to the balanced center of love, grace, and peace.

When you accept yourself as you are, you stop the mental torture you put yourself through with all the ways you tell yourself how you should be, could be, would be, have to be, ought to be, used to be, ad nauseum. You let go of your self-incriminating judgments and turn your time and attention into being your best self, meaning, you do your best and let it go at that. There's no yardstick you need to measure yourself against to see if you're good enough. Self-acceptance is about letting go of *all* the "I'm not good enough" beliefs and simply getting on with being who you are.

Elizabeth Kubler Ross was the famous author who wrote about the five stages of grief, death, and dying in her landmark book, *Of Death and Dying*. When receiving news that one's life is ending, or some other loss, we typically go through five stages, although not always in a linear fashion. These stages are: denial and isolation, anger, bargaining, depression, and acceptance. With acceptance of the inevitability of the situation, we can come to a place of inner peace.

There are always situations in life that are outside your control that require acceptance in order to have peace of mind. You cannot change the state of the world: how terrorists are exhibiting cruelty; how the government is governing, or not governing; what the stock market is doing today; or if the housing market is going to expand or decline. If you find yourself fretting over these and other situations that are out of your control, it's time to stop. Accept that "this is how it is." Forget about "how it should be." The gem for you is to find inner neutrality, accepting what is occurring. From neutrality, you can then decide if there are actions you want to take. You *respond* from *acceptance* rather than *react* from your buttons getting pushed. It's quite a different way to perceive and live life.

Even though I have chosen these five qualities and suggested you choose one to work on, in reality, that's not exactly how the spiritual path unfolds. We are all working on all of these, and many more qualities, throughout our life. We move in and out of circumstances in which we are called upon to exhibit, or more deeply embody, one trait or another – or maybe several at one time. That being said, it's still beneficial to choose one of these and spend at least the next year delving deeply into it. Make it a theme for you for the year, so that you can get to know this quality through your actions, thoughts, behaviors and emotions. Then you can decide to embody it for another year, and another year.

In the end, that's what this is all about, isn't it? We're here to learn and grow, to be all we can be. You can look at your life and see what brings you joy, what uplifts your heart, and where your passion lies. Do more of that! It's that simple – fill your life with more of what uplifts you.

As you've read through all the examples of limiting beliefs, I'm quite sure some of them have rung true with you. Understand, though, that they are just thoughts and you have the ability to move beyond the limitations your thoughts have created. Do whatever inner work is necessary to get unstuck and create new, empowering thoughts. If you have the desire, then you have the ability. My 35 years of working with clients have proven to me that we all can change our life when we change our thinking and take different actions. I've seen it happen over and over and over again.

Your life is calling to you. Pay attention to the signs that are all around and within you. Do what calls to you. You can do it! That's what creates a life-well-lived.

EMPOWERING THOUGHTS

- Be kind to yourself.

- When you tell the Universe your intention is to be kind, you will notice one or more people will come into your life to test you on your kindness skill level.

- Learning trust is an inner journey, where you connect with your soul, with your immortal self.

- You simply form the practice of being grateful for everything in your life, at all times.

- Abundance is actually not about things; it's all about consciousness.

- Anything and everything that comes into your life is an opportunity for you to grow and develop your consciousness.

- To accept a situation that is not to your liking can be difficult and challenging – but also so very, very liberating

- You accept yourself *as* you are, not how you could be or should be.

PART IV

Resources for Releasing

11

Resources

There are many ways to release old, limiting beliefs. You've been doing it all your life, so it's not new to you. As you've learned and grown, you've substituted new information for old. It can be as easy as reading a book that gives you a new perspective, a new way of looking at life that you had never considered before. You then begin to incorporate that new perspective into your life, you live it out. You're in church or synagogue and you hear something that resonates deep within you as truth, and it becomes part of how you now think and live. You take it in and use it in your everyday life. While attending a workshop or seminar, you understand a new concept and suddenly events in your life make more sense.

Every single self-help book or e-book, CD, workshop or retreat is aimed at basically the same goal: Change your thinking and you change your life. It's all about belief systems, although others may call it by different terms. Sometimes, however, your limiting beliefs are so tightly wound into your way of living and being that you can't release their impact on your own. You need assistance, a process someone else can use to help you free yourself from your limiting thinking.

The list of ways to clear out old beliefs is endless and ever changing as new approaches come to the marketplace. I'm listing different ones, most of which I've tried throughout the 35 years of doing this work. This list is by no means complete, nor does it necessarily include the "best," as though there's even a "best" way to heal. There isn't any single approach that works "best" for everyone, for every situation. Life is just not that limited. Plus, as you grow through the years, it's natural to use different types of healing modalities, or approaches, because your needs change as your consciousness grows. So what worked for you five years ago may not be what you need now.

This list is also *not* in the order of "most effective to least effective." So please don't assume that. It's just a list. Some modalities are more effective for certain types of issues, as well as for certain people. This list is a starting place. I trust you will follow your intuition and healing path to discover which approaches are right for you at different times in your life.

INDIVIDUALS REFERENCED IN THIS BOOK

(Please be aware that all web sites referenced throughout this book are accurate at the time of this writing but they may change over time.)

Braden, Gregg, www.greggbraden.com

Canning, Nancy, www.NancyCanning.com

(I have a free email series to help you find your life's calling. Also, I have special monthly CD offers, and two more books on the way! Join my mailing list to receive notice.)

Demartini, John, Dr., www.drdemartini.com

Dispenza, Joseph, Dr., www.drjoedispenza.com

Dooley, Mike, www.tut.com

Greater Good Science Center, www.greatergood.berkeley.edu

Hay House Publishing, www.hayhouse.com

Jobst, Kim, Dr., www.DrKimJobst.com and www.functionalshift.com

Katie, Byron, www.byronkatie.com and www.thework.com

Lipton, Bruce, Dr., www.brucelipton.com

Mercola, Joseph, Dr., www.drmercola.com and www.eft.mercola.com

Morrissey, Mary, www.marymorrissey.com

Myss, Caroline, www.myss.com

Proctor, Bob, www.bobproctor.com

Robson, Jon D., www.meta-medicineusa.com

Ruiz, don Miguel, www.miguelruiz.com

Searcy, Felicia B., www.feliciasearcy.com

Sheldon, Christie Marie, www.unlimitedabundance.com

Shulman, Jason, www.societyofsouls.com

Sounds True Publishing, www.soundstrue.com

Vitale, Joe, www.joevitale.com

HYPNOSIS

I start with hypnosis because that's what I've been doing for a living, so I know it best. I first learned about belief systems in 1980 from Dr. Joseph Spear in Vista, California, when he was using cassette tapes and pre-recorded hypnosis relaxation and suggestions to help clients change their beliefs.

Hypnosis isn't what most people think or expect. Many clients think you're supposed to feel "out of it" or "different." So they think they're not really in trance when they actually are – because you are clear headed, conscious and aware of what you're saying and doing while in trance. Hypnosis can be described as a state of consciousness in which the client is relaxed with eyes closed, is awake, able to speak (and walk to the bathroom, if needed), and has heightened awareness, focus, and concentration into their inner world, such as a specific memory, while blocking out distractions.

Everyone goes in and out of hypnotic trance daily. Every time you drive and don't know how you got to where you are, you've been in a light trance. Your focus was somewhere other than on driving, and yet you were able to continue to drive. You are in a trance state whenever you lose track of time watching YouTube videos, surfing the Internet, playing video games, watching sports, gardening, reading, or watching a movie. We all go in and out of trance regularly when we're falling asleep at night and waking up in the morning. It's not some mystical, magical experience. It's a natural process well known by everyone.

This modern, non-psychological definition of hypnosis from alleydog.com is amusing and nearly accurate (except for the "imaginary happenings" part):

> "Hypnosis is a temporary state of heightened relaxation and suggestibility during which some (not all) people are able to become so focused that they experience imaginary happenings as if they were real. Hypnosis is not some trans-like, magical state in which people will engage in behaviors that are completely against their 'normal, non-hypnotized' will.

> "People often believe that a hypnotist can make you do things you would never do, like take your clothes off and run around a crowded room naked. If you would not do this when you are not hypnotized, then you would not do it when you are hypnotized. However, if there is some part of you that would....well then, that may be a different story."

In a typical session, the hypnotherapist leads the client into relaxation by using induction suggestions, such as following one's breath, counting backwards, opening and closing one's eyes, fixating one's gaze on a spot on the ceiling, noticing the sensations of relaxation in the body, imagining colors moving through the chakras, guided visualization, or countless other techniques – all techniques designed to quiet one's logical mind and move the brain wave frequencies out of the waking state and into another state.

Brainwavesblog.com explains that our brains naturally produce electrical impulses that travel throughout our brains. These electrical impulses produce rhythms known as "brain waves."

How you're feeling at this given moment is a byproduct of your brain-wave activity. Every state of consciousness that you experience is a result of gamma, beta, alpha, theta, and delta brain waves. No single brain wave pattern takes over your brain at any given moment. All of them are active in your brain at all times. However, one pattern usually dominates over the others. This dominant pattern is responsible for your state of awareness.

Their web site has more information on each of these different levels of brain wave activity. Briefly defined, they are:

- Gamma brain waves: cycling at 40+ Hz are associated with problem solving in both adults and children. Gamma brain waves help you learn and sharpen your mental acuity.

- High Beta brain waves: 20 Hz - 40 Hz, are associated with fear, anxiety, excessive thinking, rapid thinking, OCD (Obsessive-Compulsive Disorder), addiction, as well as states of peak performance.

- Beta brain waves: 12 Hz - 20 Hz, are considered your "fast brain wave" activity. Each time you focus, analyze, perform calculations, or think about your external environment, beta waves are at work.

- Alpha brain waves: 8 Hz – 12 Hz, are associated with meditative states, such as visualization, hypnosis, and idleness of your optical system. Each time you daydream, relax, or close your eyes, alpha activity increases.

- Theta brain waves: 4 Hz – 7 Hz, may be rhythmic or arrhythmic. They are commonly linked to high levels of creativity, emotions, and spontaneity.

- Delta: 1 Hz – 4 Hz, are commonly associated with deep sleep and are the dominant brain wave pattern among infants.

Depending on a person's depth of relaxation, their brain waves will be in Alpha or Theta, which signifies light trance or deeper trance – but still awake. This change in brain waves enables a person, such as a hypnotherapy client, to bypass their logical, analytical mind (which is usually in control) and access their subconscious mind where 95% of consciousness is located, including subconscious beliefs, creativity, patterns, memories, and habits formed earlier in life. In this relaxed state, the client is more open to suggestions that can aid them in healing, such as retrieving a long-ago, forgotten memory, which is what makes hypnosis such a powerful transformational technique.

There are many ways to use hypnosis for healing. While in the relaxed trance state, the hypnotherapist may guide you to specific memories, give suggestions related to your goals, have you visualize your desired outcomes, or go into the past or the future to access to information to help you. Some practitioners don't engage in spoken interaction with the client during the session. Rather, they use a written script to give positive or healing suggestions to help the client resolve issues or attain specific goals. This is often the case with smoking cessation or weight management.

Hypnosis can be especially beneficial for dealing with phobias, pain management, stress, high blood pressure, during childbirth, hastening recovery from surgery and chemotherapy, reducing recovery complications, releasing traumas, and of course, releasing limiting beliefs, to name just a few.

Self-hypnosis is also highly beneficial, especially for reducing stress and visualizing goals. There are countless books and CDs on the subject, as well as YouTube videos to teach you how to relax yourself. The more you practice, the more quickly you become able to relax, and the deeper you are able to go.

One of the primary ways I work with clients in changing their limiting beliefs is to act as if each issue, habit, thought, emotion, or feeling is a little "part" – a "character" – inside them. Each part has its job, which is to be that habit or thought. For example, one part of you may want you to leave an unfulfilling job while another part of you may want you to stay because of the financial aspects.

Because our subconscious mind works in metaphors or pictures, I can use the metaphor of a "part" to talk directly with your subconscious mind, and you respond as that part within you. This may sound strange, but we actually all do this naturally. We may say, "One part of me wants to do this, but this other healthier part of me wants to do that." This is not a multiple personality disorder by any means; rather, it's called sub-personalities. We all have parts, aspects, of ourselves, and by talking to these parts, I can find out exactly when that part, or belief, was formed, what was going on at that time, the emotions felt at that time, and how the part was meant to help.

As I've noted earlier, all of this information is linked together, so it all can be accessed together very easily.

Under hypnosis, you are back in that memory at the time you formed the belief. According to your subconscious mind, you are still that three-year-old and the pain or fear is just as real in this very moment as it was then. Time is all "now" to our subconscious mind. So we are able to lead this part into present time, and help it see that it has been stuck in the subconscious mind for the past twenty, forty, or sixty years.

This aspect of this work is the most phenomenal part. There is a moment when the belief still feels so real, true, and overwhelming. You would swear it's true because you're still in the consciousness of when it was formed and felt true. Then a moment later, I lead you through pulling it away, out of the consciousness in which it was formed.

Suddenly, it all seems very silly. What was so tragic or emotional or real one moment can be fully released and resolved – becoming a non-issue – the next moment. All the energy, emotion, and strongly held thoughts are neutralized, released into the ethers, simply gone.

You can actually feel a physical shift inside yourself. Often, it feels disorienting for a time, as your mind and body reorganize into a new way of seeing the world. People usually feel lighter, as though the weight of all you have energetically been carrying is released. You can breathe more deeply and feel a sense of deep calm, peace, and serenity within.

When a belief is released, you simply no longer act or respond to life in the old way, which was the child's thinking. You now respond to life using your adult mind, logic, intuition, and knowing. It's natural and effortless. The old thought may come back, but it no longer has the charge or emotion attached to it. You can dismiss it without a second thought because you see it for what it really is: just an old thought that was never true in the first place.

This is healing, stress reduction, and deep inner peace.

EFT – EMOTIONAL FREEDOM TECHNIQUE AKA TAPPING

EFT is a form of psychological acupressure. It is based on the same energy meridians used in traditional acupuncture for over five thousand years to treat physical and emotional ailments. But EFT does not use needles. Instead, you (1) simply tap with your fingertips on specific meridian points on your head and chest, while you (2) think and speak about your specific problem and strongly feel the emotions connected with it. As you progress through the release, you begin to (4) speak positive affirmations about your desired outcome.

This combination of tapping the energy meridians, thinking and feeling the problem, while speaking positive affirmations works to clear an emotional block from your body's bioenergetic system – thereby restoring your mind and body to balance. It's a safe and gentle approach to releasing blocks in your mind, body, and emotions.

Tapping can be especially helpful with anxiety, stress, cravings, insomnia and pain, to name just a few. It has been shown to help with post-traumatic stress disorder (PTSD) because it helps remove the "short circuit" in your mind/body that keeps you revisiting the unhealthy emotions and sensations, allowing you to become calmer and more peaceful in a very short time.

Tapping is very quick and easy to learn, often taking less than 15 minutes. You can do it on your own or with another person. Children can also learn to use it. I taught it to my 12-year old great nephew to successfully eliminate anxiety about going to the dentist.

If you have serious traumas, deep emotional wounds, or medical needs, it's important to do this work with a person trained in the technique rather than just starting off on your own. Just because it's simple to learn and use, don't be fooled into thinking that it isn't powerful work. You will be amazed at what comes up within you. So find a qualified, trained practitioner to work with you through your healing journey.

Dr. Joseph Mercola is a leading expert nutritionist with an information-packed daily email that I highly recommend, www.drmercola.com. He states,

> "... keep in mind that, more than any traditional or alternative method I have used or researched, EFT works. I have witnessed the results in my patients since deciding to use EFT exclusively in June of 2001. Indeed, because of its very high rate of success, the use of EFT has spread rapidly, and medical practitioners employing EFT can now be found in every corner of the country and world."

His EFT web site, www.eft.mercola.com, leads you through the process of how to tap, the points to tap, and how to do the affirmations. There are many other online sites that give demonstrations on how to tap, as well as free scripts of affirmations. Since 2007, typically in February, there has been a free online Tapping World Summit where you are able to tap along with experts to help clear various issues. The brother and sister team, Nick and Jessica Ortner, created this summit. A few years ago I had a client email me that her back pain was gone as a result of tapping along during the program. Let's hope it continues to be available for many years to come. In 2014 they joined forces with Hay House, who sponsored their summit. www.tappingworldsummit.com.

Other well known people in the world of healing and conscious-ness growth who advocate EFT include Dr. Wayne Dyer, Louise Hay, Dr. Lissa Rankin, Jack Canfield, Kris Carr, Bob Proctor, Cheryl Richardson, Bruce Lipton, and Joe Vitale.

If you're not familiar with tapping, this may seem very strange and totally "off the wall." But I can tell you this: It works. Of course, nothing works every time for every situation for every person, but this is a powerful technique. If you read through different web sites on EFT, they state that as a result of tapping you can: improve the quality of your life; attract more money; reduce or eliminate chronic pain; feel happier; be more calm, centered, and peace-ful; sleep better; enjoy increased energy; be more creative and resourceful; improve relationships; increase your professional success; reduce cravings; and be more productive and effective.

EMDR – EYE MOVEMENT DESENSITIZATION AND REPROCESSING THERAPY

Eye Movement Desensitization and Reprocessing, or EMDR, is a powerful psychotherapy technique that has been very successful in helping people who suffer from trauma, anxiety, panic, disturb-ing memories, Post-Traumatic Stress Disorder (PTSD), and many other emotional problems. With traditional counseling, these conditions were difficult and time-consuming to treat. Extensive scientific research has shown EMDR to be a very effective and rapid method for healing PTSD and is often used with rape victims, panic attacks, veterans returning from war, witnesses to traumatic events, and other highly charged emotional memories.

Unlike EFT Tapping, which can be utilized with minimal time and training, EMDR should be administered only by qualified, trained professionals because it includes an entire eight-phase protocol and is used in conjunction with other therapeutic approaches. It's a simple, yet extremely powerful tool for bringing quick and lasting relief for most types of emotional distress.

You can think of EMDR as "erasing" the charged emotions and memories. When you use an eraser on a piece of paper, you go back and forth with the eraser as the image disappears. EMDR is similar in that – as you bring to mind the highly charged memory and feel the associated emotions – you move your eyes right to left, following the finger (or wand) of the therapist as it moves. Right/left, right/left, right/left for 20-30 seconds or more. It's like watching a game of tennis, your eyes moving back and forth following the ball. The more vividly you can see and feel the memory, the more easily it can resolve quickly.

Using EMDR, people "erase" the memory by activating the opposite sides of their brain, releasing the emotional experiences trapped in their nervous system. In addition to the eye movement, therapists can use auditory tones, tapping on the knees, holding balls that alternately vibrate, and other right/left stimulations.

As the charge of the emotions is released, the associated beliefs and thoughts, such as *"I'm to blame,"* are also released and replaced by new, calmer, more appropriate thoughts and emotions. According to the EMDR Institute, after EMDR processing, clients generally report that the emotional distress related to the memory has been eliminated, or greatly decreased, and that they have gained important cognitive insights. Importantly, these emotional and cognitive changes usually result in spontaneous behavioral and personal change, which are further enhanced with standard EMDR procedures.

VISUALIZATION / GUIDED IMAGERY

Visualization, also called guided imagery, mental imagery, or performance imagery, involves using your mind to clearly picture a desired outcome or goal while also vividly feeling the emotions and sensations associated with having that desired outcome. You repeatedly imagine how you want to be while feeling what it's like to be that way.

This technique has been shown to be powerful in creating life changes. It's been well documented to be one of the main tools that enable athletes to become top performers.

According to sports psychologist Terry Orlick, author of *In Pursuit of Excellence*, many Olympic athletes credit their success to daily visualizations; they see themselves as winning the gold medal long before they ever achieve it. Orlick stresses the importance of visualization, saying, "Athletes who make the fastest progress and those who ultimately become their best make extensive use of performance imagery." Orlick speaks of training the mind and body to execute skills to perfection by programming a high-quality performance into the athlete's brain.

While visualization is a power mind tool, many times people think that it's enough to just visualize what they want without actually doing the action. In sports, visualization *supplements* the athlete's inherent skill, expert coaching, and rigorous training regimens.

Changing your beliefs or taking on new behaviors requires a multi-pronged approach. You visualize in your mind doing the behavior you desire. Let's say you're afraid of speaking in public, and you realize your fear is holding you back professionally. Your beliefs may be, *"I'm going to make a fool of myself, I won't know what to say, I'll get all tongue-tie, and I'm going to die right up on stage."* If you *even* think of speaking to a group, your heart may beat faster, your palms get sweaty, your stomach ties itself into knots, and you feel light-headed. This is the mind-body connection at work within you.

When you think of speaking in front of a group, your subconscious mind can take over. It checks what it knows to be true about speaking in public and begins sending messages throughout your body that correspond to the your own personal belief systems. In your case, it creates the physical fear-based sensations and thoughts of *"I just can't do it."*

You can use this same mind-body connection in your favor to override your fear-based image.

Mentally imagine yourself speaking to a group, feeling confident, assured, articulate, knowledgeable, and successful. Really, really feel it, and picture it vividly. It's not enough to just sort of see it in your mind's eye. That's not enough energy to begin to diffuse and replace your old neuro-pathways of fear.

The emotions you feel in these new visualizations need to be strong enough to outweigh the old fearful emotions. It's not enough to just repeat *"I am a confident public speaker"* one hundred times a day without seeing, feeling, and living it in your mind.

So, be there. See and feel yourself standing in front of an audience. Enjoy the command you have over the audience, how they are focused on you (not their cell phones). Luxuriate in the exhilaration of words just naturally flowing out of your mouth. Feel amazingly articulate. Sense the audience responding positively. You can hear a pin drop. They are silent to catch your every word. Be in that moment. Live it. Stand up straight. Gesture appropriately.

Feel your calmness and your thrill. Feel your body sensations. This is you.

In the beginning, you will be "faking" all this in your mind, of course. But that's the point. You picture yourself appearing in front of a group the way you *want* to be, not the way you are now. When you feel it intensely and vividly, as you do this exercise repeatedly, you will notice positive changes in your visualizations. You will more easily picture and feel the new way of being. Your excitement, and self-confidence, will rise as your old fears become less prominent, fading away.

Also, take action on your visualization. Perhaps go to a speaking club, such as Toastmasters or Speaking Circles, based on Lee Glickstein's book, *Be Heard Now*. In these groups you get to actually begin to do the work – in positive and supportive circumstances.

Or make it a point to speak up in meetings at work, especially if you would have remained silent in the past. Practice with friends; speak your mind more freely and openly if that has not been your pattern. Do something, anything, to practice and put your new behaviors into action. Visualization is part of the shifting process. Actually doing the new behavior is the final outcome.

My sister had such a huge fear of speaking in front of a class in high school that she purposely took the long way between classes to avoid walking past the speech classroom – for fear that a hand would reach out and pull her into that room. It took her 25 more years to become receptive enough to go to a Toastmasters' meeting – at the urging of our mother. Mom had joined Toastmasters and loved it so much, and piled up so many speaking trophies, that she was sure my sister would love it also. Sure enough, my sister cautiously went to Toastmasters, worked at her speeches, and showed up almost every week for 13 years. She was even president of the club twice, and won a few trophies. But her real trophy was losing her fear of public speaking. She became comfortable not only speaking in front of a group but also leading it. Her continual practice did it. You don't have to wait as long as she did.

Or, take another approach, if you're one of the many people who thinks *"I can't visualize."* Pretend you're seeing something, imagine it in your mind as though you're actually seeing that thing. It's a practice, and you can get better at it.

It's very possible that you just have a belief that you can't visualize; therefore, you don't see much in your mind. However, think about your living room, or a pet, or a grandchild you love. Can you picture them or see them in your mind or feel them in your heart? Notice how that image of a loved one or a space you know well comes to mind. That's how you visualize. So do the same with desired outcomes. Feel the love you have for your pet or your grandchild and transfer that emotion to a scene you bring to mind of how you want to be.

Yet another way to visualize a "future you" is to have a hypnotherapist, or another person trained in guided imagery, take you on a guided imagery "adventure."

The technique I use is to have my clients sit in a comfortable relaxed position, close their eyes, and, as they listen to me describe the scene, see it in their mind's eye. I first talk them through relaxing their body, starting with their head, feeling their mouth and eyes relax, then their neck and shoulders, on down to their toes.

Then I tell them that they are at the top of a down escalator, and they will relax even further as the escalator takes them down, down, as I count down from ten to one. At the bottom, I describe the scene they are in.

One of my favorite people for teaching the power of visualization is Mike Dooley, creator of www.tut.com and author of *Infinite Possibilities*. He sends out a daily email in which he speaks as "The Universe," reminding those of us who subscribe (for free) to visualize, imagine, see it clearly, take small steps, and thereby create our vision. His messages start me off each day with encouragement, humor, and spiritual teaching. He also offers workshops around the world, and has trained practitioners in his methods of creation. I've been to one of his workshops and I believe he's "the real deal."

Your mind is far more powerful than you give it credit for – far more powerful. It's your thoughts that are the limiting factor, not your brain or your ability to visualize.

MEDITATION

Have you ever wondered why all the major spiritual traditions throughout time advocate meditation or some form of getting quiet and going within oneself? Could it be that it works? When I take people into deep hypnosis and into the spirit world, one piece of wisdom that is consistent throughout all the afterlife journeys is "meditate." Get quiet and listen to your inner voice.

When you meditate – as with hypnosis, guided visualization, and prayer – your brain waves change from the alert Beta waves down to the more relaxed Alpha waves. That means that the frequency of your brain waves decrease and your brain activity slows down. When this happens, you are able to access your subconscious mind and inner knowing. In this state, you can effect change within yourself by simply listening to your inner voice. If you don't hear anything, just be patient and listen to your breath. Just keep following your breath in and out, and then move your attention to your heart and be aware of the beating of your heart. This exercise, in and of itself, is healing and transformative.

There are many different types of meditation and I won't begin to describe them all here. If you are new to meditation, I highly encourage you to take a meditation class so that you are being guided into the inner state. It's also helpful to hear the experience and questions of others in the class.

You may think, "I don't have an extra hour every morning!" so I just don't have the time. Don't start with an hour, then. Start with five minutes. Five minutes. You have five minutes. We all have five minutes. Before you jump out of bed, lie there for five minutes and follow your breath, quiet your mind from thinking about all you have to do during the day. There's plenty of time for that planning later. For now, for those first five minutes, give yourself the gift of a quiet mind. Then add in doing the same practice before falling off to sleep. With time, you'll naturally increase it to ten minutes, and then let your inner knowing guide you in your daily practice.

Yes, I did say "daily" practice. Meditation is like any other health regimen, such as brushing our teeth or washing our face. It becomes a way of starting and/or ending our day.

WORKSHOPS AND RETREATS

There's nothing quite like spending several days in the presence of like-minded individuals who are also intent on changing their lives. The power of the group's energy can enable you to make massive changes, compared to sitting alone at home reading a book about it. Plus, you have the experience of meeting others, making new friends, adding to the quality of your life.

There are far too many retreat centers in the U.S. and around the world to begin to mention; any list would be sorely incomplete. If you don't know where to start, begin at the websites of some of your favorite personal growth and self-improvement authors; see where they are speaking or leading workshops. One thing will lead to the next. That's how flow happens. Use your intuition and jump into a new experience that excites you.

If you are in an isolated location, with no workshops near you, then opt for online seminars. There are countless free online seminars happening all the time. They typically last for a week or more and feature anywhere from 15 to 115 experts in the field, each talking for an hour. Typically, there is little or no registration fee because all the authors or speakers are selling their products at reduced rates, and they have your email for future sales. It's a powerful way to gain access to top leaders in the field of personal development from the comfort of your own computer.

The other way to access workshop information is through the facilitator's web site by purchasing their CDs or DVDs or downloads. I especially like Christie Marie Sheldon's Unlimited Abundance (www.unlimitedabundance.com) program of 24 lessons that she recorded during an online class she gave. She combines connecting to Source, energy clearing, and visualization to clear your blocks to creating abundance. The techniques she uses bring together many different tools I've studied over the years, and I've found her work to be very helpful. I listen to the different lessons repeatedly and have seen definite positive results in my life.

BOOKS AND MORE

While there are many publishers who offer metaphysical books, the leader in this field is Hay House Publishing, www.hayhouse. com. They offer far more than just books; they also have CDs, DVDs, movies, calendars, an online radio program, seminars, workshops, their annual online Hay House World Summit, and their I Can Do It! Conferences held throughout the year in various locations.

Sounds True Publishing, www.soundstrue.com, has also been in the business for decades. It offers more than 500 audio, video, and music titles about spiritual traditions, meditation, psychology, creativity, health, as well as online radio.

All of your favorite authors have their own websites where you will find books, workshops, online seminars, CDs, DVDs, live question-and-answer offerings, and much more. There is a wealth of information available to you, sometimes at no cost, sometimes at great cost.

It is so good to be alive at this time when there is such a wealth of information and spiritual enrichment available at our fingertips to all of us around the world.

EMPOWERING THOUGHTS

- Every single self-help book or e-book, CD, workshop or retreat is aimed at basically the same goal: Change your thinking and you change your life.

- Suddenly, it all seems very silly. What was so tragic or emotional or real one moment can be fully released and resolved – becoming a non-issue – the next moment.

- Tapping is very quick and easy to learn, often taking less than 15 minutes.

- EMDR should be administered only by qualified, trained professionals.

- Visualization has been well documented to be one of the main tools that enable athletes to become top performers.

- Start with five minutes of meditation. Five minutes. You have five minutes.

ABOUT THE AUTHOR

Nancy Canning has worked with thousands of clients since 1980, helping them transform and improve the quality of their lives. She loves her work and feels honored to be part of the healing journey of so many people, from so many places, including England, Egypt, the USA, Canada, Sweden, Ireland, Spain, Portugal, Columbia, Mexico, China, Vietnam, Japan, Australia, and the Philippines. Nancy offers private sessions in person, on the phone, and via Skype. Visit her web site, www.NancyCanning.com, for details and to arrange a session.

She has her Master's Degree in counseling psychology, is a certified clinical hypnotherapist, international workshop facilitator, engaging teacher, trained psychic, and is certified in past lives and journeys into the afterlife. Her first book, *Past to Present: How Your Past Lives Are Impacting You* helps people understand how their previous lives still influence them today. It's an eye-opening read. She is also a co-author of *The Inspiration Bible: The Unseen Force Transforming Lives Worldwide*.

Nancy offers the unique perspective of how one's past lives, in between lives, and this life all combine to create one's life lessons and purpose. She offers various free email series on her web site, as well as notices about special events and upcoming classes.

She has two more books percolating within her, coming into physical manifestation in 2015 and beyond. Their intent is to help people live a life worthy of their dreams and their soul's purpose.